Commandos on Death's Door
NATO's Kosovo Special Response Force

Yves Debay

Excellent view of 8ème RPIMa paratroopers deploying along the desolate Balkan landscape. They are armed with FAMAS 5.56mm assault rifles, FR-F2 sniper rifles, and the now ubiquitous Minimi 5.56mm light machine gun.

"NATO's military action supports the political aims of the international community: a peaceful multi-ethnic, democratic Kosovo in which all its people live in security...The Federal Republic of Yugoslavia must stop all repressive and combat activity and withdraw its forces from Kosovo under the protection of an international security force." - NATO spokesman Jamie Shea

The legacy of the Balkans has been written in the blood of the millions who died thinking they could control, let alone conquer, the inescapable hell of that bitter and unforgiving landscape. The ethnic divisions are not mere hatreds that have turned to armed conflict. The divisions are an unstoppable loathing that is part and parcel of every Serb, Kosovar, Croat, Macedonian, Montenegrin, and Bosnian. It is what defines who they are and whom they must avenge. Ethnic hatred is the blood and soul of the Balkans. It is as much an element of the geography as are the towns, mountains and villages of the Balkans. Nowhere is this bloodstained geography more evident than in Kosovo, the ground zero of Serbian nationalism and a flash point of autonomous yearning that has pitted historic blood enemies in a battle of mass murder, guerrilla warfare and ethnic cleansing. Stepping into the fray, however, is NATO and the world's most powerful military alliance. In an attempt to reverse a determined effort by Yugoslav President Slobodan Milosevic to once-and-for-all purge Kosovo of its dominant Albanian-majority, NATO has drawn a line in the blood-red hills of the Balkans that mass-murder and mass-expulsion will simply not be tolerated. When NATO crosses that line, it will be the elite of the alliance that will race into the fray.

Kosovo has, for centuries, been claimed by many different nationalities, often as a buffer protecting one ethnic group in the Balkans from the other. The Serbs consider it the cradle of their nation, the site of an epic battle in the fourteenth-century that defines the Serb nation. The calls to ethnically cleanse the ninety-percent Muslim Albanian population from its territory have become the political cornerstone on which the nationalists and ultra-nationalists in Belgrade are now defining the fragmented and Serb-led Republic of Yugoslavia. In 1459, Serbia fell to the Turks. The Serb thirst to right the wrong of history has lasted to this day.

Following the end of the Second World War Marshal Tito's skillful—and repressive—measures had taped the fractured ethnic divide of the Yugoslav Republic into a unified nation. Yet even through Tito's reign, the issue of Kosovo and its ethnic imbalance remain unsettled. Kosovar, or ethnic Albanian, demands for republic status within the federation were continuous, however, and sporadic Serb crackdowns were common and brutal. The province's status changed in 1974 when the new Yugoslav Constitution removed Kosovo from direct political dominance by Serbs and proclaimed it an autonomous province of the federal republic. Yet following the death of Tito in 1980, acts of civil disorder and economic sabotage, led largely by students at the University of Pristina, in Kosovo's capital city, escalated to a point where the province was soon occupied by the Yugoslav People's Army.

Italian troopers look on as a flight of A-129 Mangustas are prepared on the flight line at Petrovac airfield. Armed with TOW missiles and 68mm rocket pods, the Mangustas are formidable aerial killing machines, with combat experience in the hell of Somalia where the choppers scored several "kills," reducing the "Technical Car" armed pick-ups used by the local militiamen into vaporized balls of flames.

Close-up view of the innovative A-129 design—a sleek and combat proven airborne fire platform.

A tandem of A-129 Mangustas prepares to patrol the precarious frontier near Kosovo.

An Italian Agusta Bell-412 from the 1st Regiment Aves Antares patrols a sector while flying a medevac mission for the Extraction Force.

For many in NATO, veterans who served in the former Yugoslavia first in Croatia and Bosnia Herzegovina, and then in Macedonia, the handwriting had been on the wall for quite sometime that Kosovo would be the next major Balkan flash-point. In 1989, Belgrade rescinded Kosovo's "special status"; President Slobodan Milosevic revoked Kosovo's autonomy in keeping with his ultra-right wing campaign pledge to create a "Greater Serbia." Serb police and military units, acting on direct president directives from Belgrade, initiated a brutal campaign of killings and rapes designed to force the Kosovars from their homes once and for all. The Kosovo Liberation Army, the KLA or UCK (as they are known in Albanian), a rag-tag guerrilla formation that vowed to achieve independence for Kosovo, initiated a hit-and-run campaign designed to prove to the Serbs that a war of annihilation would be costly.

In the summer of 1998, the Yugoslav military answered the increasingly lethal Kosovo Liberation Army's guerrilla campaign for independence from Serbia with a harsh offensive against the region's ethnic Albanian majority. Serb forces attacked the civilian population with brutal ferocity. Villages were destroyed and hundreds of thousands forced to leave their home and seek shelter in Albania or Macedonia. The slaughter was wholesale and NATO vowed that it would not repeat the mistakes made in Bosnia and sit idly by as a nation was butchered. NATO and United Nations and, primarily, Organization for Security and Cooperation in Europe (OSCE) mediators, diplomats and strategists attempted to seek a political solution to the conflict, yet the 700 years of enmity, blood-vengeance and intolerance could not be resolved courtesy of even the most noble of intentions. A wider war, one involving the

entire NATO alliance, seemed unavoidable. The threatened war over Kosovo, the war against Slobodan Milosevic, would be NATO's first.

In October, under threat of NATO air strikes, Milosevic signed a cease-fire agreement with U.S. envoy Richard Holbrooke. The diplomats had attempted to press the Serbs and the KLA to forge a peaceful arrangement to end the bloodshed, but nothing in the Balkans ever go as planned or as hoped. By January 1999, the situation had deteriorated to full-fledged carnage. The massacre of forty-five Kosovar civilians by Serb forces in the village of Racak signaled the failure of Holbrooke's cease-fire. In February, NATO sponsored a "shotgun wedding" diplomatic last-chance for peace in Kosovo when it demanded that both sides meet in France and sign on to a Western-authored peace deal or face a military response. Two weeks of talks at Rambouillet, France failed to produce anything other than lost opportunity. Both the Serbs and the ethnic Albanians refused to sign a deal. The Serbs escalated the crisis by launching another large-scale offensive in Kosovo.

Yet long before the first NATO warplanes zeroed in on Serb targets inside Kosovo and throughout Yugoslavia to commence "Operation Allied Force," in the largest aerial assault since Operation Desert Storm, NATO had been poised for ground operation inside Kosovo and beyond. The NATO Extraction Force was a contingency military entity designed to intervene in an instant should OSCE or other NATO and United Nations personnel be held hostage or placed in danger. According to an agreement signed October 16, 1998, Belgrade assumed the *primary* responsibility for the safety and security of the OSCE mission and its

A French Gazelle from 3ème RHC flies a sortie within eyeshot of Serb antiaircraft gunners. Used for various missions, including reconnaissance and C³ roles, the Gazelles are armed with 20mm cannons.

A CH-47D Chinook from the Royal Netherlands Air Force's 298th Squadron operates with a force of French paratroopers as both forces hones its heliborne insertion skills near the Kosovo border.

A Puma from 3ème RHC deploys on a supply run to units positioned "eyeball-to-eyeball" with Serb forces along the Kosovo frontier. The Pumas, venerable workhorses, are the premier helicopter transports in use by the Extraction Force.

During an operational exercise, a platoon of French paratroopers races toward the cargo door of a CH-47D. The number of fully equipped troopers who use the hulking chopper for aerial transport ideally illustrates the sheer cargo capacity of the CH-47. Called the "Mini-Hercules" by many of the French soldiers who work with the Dutch in the Extraction Force, most infantrymen appreciate the wide-spaces and smooth flight of the CH-47.

timeline toward possible NATO military intervention was fast and furious:

- September 23 1998: The United Nations Security Council adopts Resolution 1199, which demands to all parties to end hostilities and maintain a cease-fire in Kosovo.
- October 12, 1998: NATO's highest decision-making authority, the North Atlantic Council (NAC), issues an activation order allowing for limited air strikes and a phased air campaign (Operation Determined Force) if Yugoslav authorities refuse to comply with the UN demands.
- October 15, 1998: Yugoslav President Milosevic commits to cease hostilities, withdraw mobilized forces in Kosovo and accept international verification of compliance.
- October 24, 1998: The United Nations Security Council adopts Resolution 1203, which endorses and supports both OSCE and NATO verification missions.
- October 30, 1998: The NAC approves the execution of Operation Eagle Eye.
- November 13, 1998: The NAC approves the plan for Operation Joint Guarantor.
- November 26, 1998: The Kosovo Verification Coordination Center is formally established at Kumanovo, Macedonia.
- December 4, 1998: The NAC approves the execution of Operation Joint Guarantor.
- December 6, 1998: Deployment of Extraction Force elements to FYROM begins.
- December 10, 1998: The Headquarters of the Extraction Force is activated at Kumanovo.
- January 15, 1999: The Extraction Force is fully operational.

The Extraction Force is composed primarily of European units, with France serving as the vanguard force and lead military contributor. The

Extraction Force's headquarters, along with rapid response team, are all stationed in Macedonia and comprises nearly 2,500 soldiers. Their mission, "Operation Determined Guarantor," ostensibly a protection force to safeguard European monitors in Yugoslavia, has placed the Extraction Force in the front line of NATO's war against the Serbs.

The contributing forces to "Operation Determined Guarantor" include:

- **France:** A headquarter and paratroop company of 8ème RPIMa (*Regiment de Parachutiste d'Infanterie de Marine*), a force of helicopters from 3ème RHC (*Regiment d'Hélicoptère de Combat*) with four Gazelles and eight Pumas.
- **Germany:** A paratroop company from the 314th *Fallschirmjäger* Battalion with thirty-two armored vehicles (Fuchs and Luchs).
- **Netherlands:** Three CH-47D Chinook helicopters; an engineer company; and, a squadron of ambulances.
- **Italy:** Task Force "Garibaldi" consisting of a motorized infantry company (the 8th *Bersaglieri*) and two armored platoons (19th *Cavalleggeri* Guide) along with an attack-chopper element with four A-129 Mangusta and two AB-412 choppers.
- **United Kingdom:** A mechanized company, complete with twelve Warrior APCs and four FV-432s with 81mm mortar, led by the King's Own Royal Border Regiment.

Being large and slow makes the CH-47D a juicy-target for antiaircraft gunners—mounted .50 caliber machine gun is a lethal equalizer to most ground threats.

French paratroopers from 8ème RPIMa deploy from an Aérospatiale AS 332 Super Puma during exercises along the Kosovo frontier.

French paratroop squad commander makes sure that his men are inside the cargo hold of their Aérospatiale AS 332 Super Puma "in a hurry" as they complete a patrol of the Kosovo border area.

Racing from cover to cover, a French sniper moves into firing position, wearing the new French military camouflage and body armor perfected during the years of UN service in Bosnia.

French paratroopers, deploying from their VBL (Vehicule Blindé Léger), move into position as they prepare a roadblock. During joint-exercises with the Germans in which they are role-playing as "the Serbs," both forces hone their skills at stopping enemy vehicles at checkpoints.

A French sniper, armed with a FR-F2 7.62mm sniper rifle, checks with his commander before selecting a few "interesting" targets across the frontier. Note the rough terrain near the Kosovo/Macedonia frontier in which any NATO ground operations against the Serbs will have to be fought.

Stoic portrait of a 8ème RPIMa paratroop officer, armed with the FAMAS 5.56mm assault rifle.

A typical 8ème RPIMa sniper team consists of one observer and two marksmen, one armed with a 12.7mm Hecate heavy sniper rifle and the other a FR-F2. The FR-F2 is usually used for targets in a range of 500 to 800 meters away, with the Hecate used for ranges from 800 to 1800 meters. Nevertheless, as the French learned in Bosnia, the 12.7mm sniper rifle presents a daunting challenge that strikes fear into the hearts of any enemy, as it is lighter but more powerful than the McMillan .50 caliber sniper rifle.

8ème RPIMa paratroopers man a sniper position near Kumanovo—the sniper armed with a 7.62mm FR-F2 and the lead gunner peering through the sights of his 12.7mm Hecate "heavy sniping rifle."

A paratroop sergeant checks the scores of "his" snipers during some practice work on the range.

French paratroopers, playing the role of Serb policemen with the skill of a Hollywood veteran, stop a German Luchs and Fuchs armored reconnaissance patrol at a roadblock.

Attempting to mimic the behavior and demeanor of a Serb police officer, a French paratroop officer refuses to allow a German armored reconnaissance force entry at a roadblock during exercises meant to see just how "Extraction Force" units would respond if turned away at the frontier by Serb forces.

French and German forces engage in a nail-biting game of "Chicken" as they engage in a stubborn game of "stop and go" meant to replicate what any move into Kosovo or Serbia might be like.

A French sniper peers through the scope of his FR-F2 7.62mm precision rifle. French snipers, considered among the finest in Europe, served brilliantly in the hell of Bosnia and are now poised to once again prove their eagle-eye skills.

A French sapper from the 17ème RGP (Régiment de Génie Parachutiste) utilizes his Matra low-pressure anti-mine equipment as he attends to several "unidentified devices."

A 17ème RGP sapper displays the unique attributes of his Matra low-pressure anti-mine equipment as he gingerly walks through an area deemed "unsafe" by Macedonian authorities near the frontier with Kosovo. With experience in Chad, Lebanon, Kuwait, Afghanistan, Cambodia and Bosnia, 17ème RGP combat engineers are among the most experienced in the world. And, in any future ground conflagration involving NATO in Kosovo, their talents and skills will be invaluable.

Gebirgsjägers from the 223rd Regiment, an element of the German contribution to the Extraction Force led by the 314th Fallschirmjäger Battalion, take advantage of some down time to hone their skills on the range with their G-36.

A French team of surveyors and intelligence officers from a geographic battalion sets up a portable GPS (Global Positioning Satellite) system only a few miles from the frontier in order to update existing road maps being issued by the French military for possible use in any Kosovo operation. The Army VLRA VLISS truck, which fields highly-sophisticated mapping and targeting tools, is deployed close to front line units in order to pinpoint targets, help avoid friendly fire incidents in the often confusing mountainous terrain of Kosovo, and to assist medevac teams in reaching hard-hit troops in arduous locations.

A Gebirgsjäger *operator peers through the sights of his Heckler and Koch G-36 assault rifle. He is complete with his Kevlar helmet and obligatory goggles.*

Stoic portrait of a Gebirgsjäger *lieutenant and platoon commander pleased at the impressive scores his troopers have achieved on the range. The photograph shows to advantage the new German load-bearing equipment developed specifically for the new global military-minded missions of the German military.*

A Gebirgsjäger *sniper takes aim with his G-22 7.62mm sniper's rifle. A copy of the British L-96 A1, the G-22 is a sturdy weapon that many of Germany's elite force find of superior quality—especially in the harsh climactic and geographic conditions of the Balkans.*

"Any Tangos in the cross-hairs will be terminated!" With the poise and position of a master, a young Gebirgsjäger *sniper takes aim with his G-22.*

Fallschirmjägers *from the 314th Battalion provide close-protection to a fleet of Spähpanzer Luchs reconnaissance vehicles.*

A squadron of Spähpanzer Luchs reconnaissance vehicles from the German 120th Aufklärung Kompanie *moves out along a forest clearing. The Luchs patrol a darkened stretch of roadway near the border with Kosovo cognizant of the fact that a routine patrol can become an explosive dash across the frontier.*

Like the cartoon character after who this Spähpanzer Luchs reconnaissance vehicle is named, the crew of this armored car hopes that it too will never be caught and never find itself in the sights of a Serb anti-tank team.

German combat engineers deploy from a Fuchs armored car as they search roadways along the frontier for any mines planted by Serb special forces.

Every forty-eight hours, intelligence officers from the German 7th Artillery Regiment launch a CL-289 drone for a reconnaissance sortie over Serb positions in Kosovo.

Close-up view of the CL-289 drone—one of the most valuable real-time combat tools available for ground troops poised for operation inside Kosovo.

Mine-clearing work is tedious, nerve-racking and dangerous beyond words. Needless to say that it takes a unique breed of individual to voluntarily take on such work and the sappers from Britain's Royal Engineers are among the best in the world.

Specialists from the Royal Engineers receive an additional briefing as well as equipment prior to embarking on a mine-clearing exercise close to the frontier.

Warrior APCs from "Burma Company," 1st Battalion, King's Own Royal Border Regiment, prepare for a deployment close to the often indistinguishable frontier with Kosovo. Maintenance is a religious reality practiced by all "Extraction Force" personnel.

Armed with Enfield L86 5.56mm squad support weapons, troopers from the King's Own Royal Border Regiment endures the frosty Balkan afternoon after an exhausting weeklong exercise in the field.

Months of winter, rain, snow and wind, along with routine patrolling and exercises can take its toll on an armored fighting vehicle, even one designed to withstand 100mm cannons and RPGs.

The reality of a Balkan winter is snow, bone-numbing cold, and the reality that combat does not get time off due to bad weather.

The snow-capped shrubbery and the majestic hills are a beguiling first-impression that many receive during a first trip to the Balkans in winter. But the terrain and picturesque landscape are merely a camouflage. There is nothing charming about a part of the world where hatred and murder have become the currency of day-to-day existence.

Mud, cold and danger—a Balkans primer.

An FV-432 81mm mortar vehicle moves into position in order to provide close artillery support to British troopers operating close to Serb lines.

Close-up view of the 81mm mortar firing area on a FV-432 APC.

Dismounted troopers of the 19th Cavalleggeri Guide from Task Force Garibaldi, a cavalry element equipped with Type 6614 VBLs, deploy along a stretch of Macedonian countryside. Task Force Garibaldi's primary mission is long-range reconnaissance, though its operators are also tasked with espionage sorties behind enemy lines.

Close-up view of a British mortar team commander as he receives firing coordinates from front-line spotters.

A reconnaissance scout from Task Force Garibaldi scopes out a target on his AR70/90 5.56mm assault rifles.

Interesting portrait of the weaponry and gear carried by Italian 19th Cavalleggeri Guide troopers in battle. The AR/90 assault rifle has proven itself, both in Somalia and Bosnia, as a reliable and accurate weapon.

During predawn exercises near the Kosovo border, elements from Task Force Garibaldi seize a bridge. If the Extraction Force is sent into Kosovo, there will be lots of bridges and obstacles that will require a lightning fast military solution.

Interesting photograph of the improvised ballistic shields afforded to Centauro turret gunners as they patrol a section very close to Serb lines in Kosovo.

Stoic portrait of an Italian 19th Cavalleggeri Guide's Centauro armored car commander in action.

The impressive and daunting Centauro has, in action in Bosnia with SFOR, proven to be the mightiest of armored cars. For Operation Determined Guarantor, NATO planners realize that the Centauros will be tasked with punching a hole through the Serb's first line of defense. Note the business end of the 105mm main armament cannon that makes the Centauro such a lethal—and mobile—combat vehicle.

Tradition and heroics are a Bersaglieri Company calling card. Amid the mud and tensions of the Balkan tinderbox, a Bersaglieri operator wears his helmet with characteristic feather in the true tradition of how the unit has always deployed into harm's way.

Mechanized infantrymen from the elite Italian 8th Bersaglieri Company respond to an ambush during a training exercise as they protect the vehicles in their convoy along a section of paved roadway in the outer stretches of the Macedonian border area.

Italian sapper prepares for a combat mission to clear a field of enemy ordnance along the border with Kosovo during a training exercise. Such a realistic training exercise meant to replicate what any first push into Kosovo will be like

NATO at Kosovo's Door
Cooperative Best Effort 98

Yves Debay

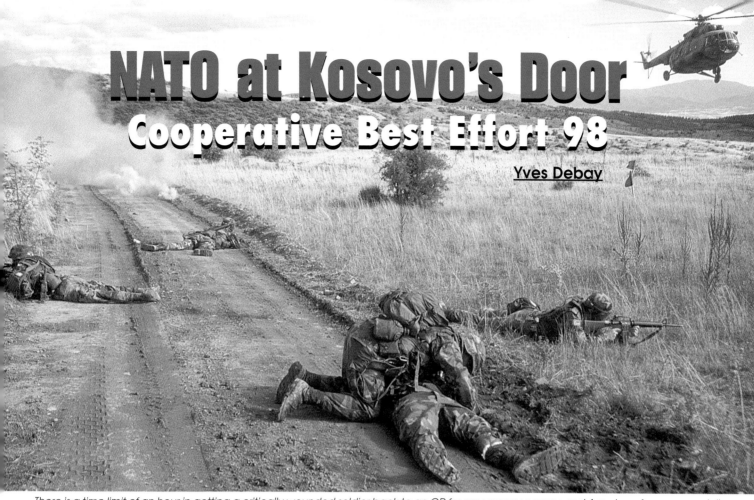

There is a time limit of an hour in getting a critically wounded soldier back to an OR for emergency surgery, and American forces, especially those assigned to peace-keeping missions, perfect their evacuation and emergency medical procedure skills with zealous dedication. Under "fire" and nearly out of time, if the wounded personnel will receive proper emergency medical treatment, soldiers from the 1st Infantry Division call in a medevac, a Macedonian Air Force Mi-17 chopper, during Phase III of "Cooperative Best Effort '98."

Dateline February 11, 1999: Racak, Serbia. On a bone-numbing winter's morning, amid the howling of the eastern winds and the unmistakable silence of a snow-covered town, the bodies of forty Kosovo Albanians, men women and children butchered in cold-blood, were finally laid to rest. The massacre of the forty, a crime so reprehensible that it sparked the NATO allies to finally demand a political settlement to this, the latest tinderbox in the Balkans, led to the scheduled peace talks in France. William Walker, the Kosovo verification chief whose denunciation of the killings three weeks ago as a "massacre" focused world attention to the unabridged savagery was quoted as saying that

Moldavian troopers from the 1st Infantry Brigade simulate the evacuation of a wounded civilian in a "fictitious" village that was the victim of a massacre.

Like many of the Eastern European nations, or those emerging directly from the Soviet Empire, these Moldavian soldiers wear and carry a combination of Eastern Bloc gear and weaponry, and more luxurious equipment obtained from the West.

As the "wounded civilian" is carried back to an aid station, a Moldavian infantryman covers the withdrawal with his AK assault rifle.

An Albanian security trooper, armed with a Chinese long-barreled knock-off of the AK-47 and wearing fatigues obtained through emergency American aid, is poised for action during a convoy exercise.

"Cooperative Best Effort '98" was designed to serve as a platform in which soldiers from the have and have-not nations could act as one. Here, an Albanian trooper (from a have-not country as exists in Europe) conducts patrol exercises with his counterparts from the United States, Great Britain and France.

"evil had visited Racak." Nearly 10,000 people, some having survived massacres of their own villages, crowded around the central mosque, some twenty miles south of the capital Pristina, to pay their final respects and show the world that bloodshed would not be forgotten and, unless a Solomon-like peace arrangement fostered between the Serbs and the Kosovo Albanians, the victims would be avenged.

Finding a solution to the minefield that is Kosovo will not be easy—the look on the faces of several fighters and commanders from the Kosovo Liberation Army (KLA) attending the funerals in Racak was pure vengeance. For the forces on the ground, let alone the victims of wholesale slaughter, the diplomatic offensive in France provided little hope for a peaceful resolution to the centuries of hatred. After all, for generations Kosovo has been a territory disputed between Serbs and Albanians with a blood score to settle. Albanians claim that they are the sole legitimate masters of the land; they claim that they are descendants of the ancient Illyrians and that the beleaguered province is theirs by birthright. The Serbs, on the other hand, say that Kosovo is at the heart of its grand medieval kingdom. A key date in Kosovo's history is June 28, 1389, when according to Serbian history, the Serbs fought the invading Ottoman Turks at Kosovo Polje and lost. But ancient history is of little importance to NATO commanders, and officials in Washington D.C., London, Paris and Rome. They saw Kosovo, a desolate mountainous area with few natural resources other than unyielding hatred, as just the type of post-Cold War ethnic conflict that could, if unchecked, create an unstoppable chain of events that could propel much of Europe into full-scale war.

NATO had learned its costly lesson of high-brow indifference during the first Balkan War of the 1990s. In Kosovo, the Western powers and their new Eastern Europe allies, were not about to make the same mistakes twice. In 1998, in the area surrounding Kosovo, NATO special forces teams engaged in a deliberate exercise meant to send a resounding message to both the Serbs and the ethnic Albanian, that military intervention could be hard and swift. That message was "Cooperative Best Effort '98."

On the week of September 11, 1998 the Macedonian town of Krivolak was host to a remarkable gathering by military units from twenty-six nations in a NATO exercise code-named "Cooperative Best Effort" designed to evaluate infantry readiness for the irregular warfare hell that can be a conflict in the Balkans. "Cooperative Best Effort," a noble and grand-scale international military attempt at forceful peace-keeping was carried out only 100 kilometers south of Kosovo, where ethnic Albanians from the KLA and conventional Serb military forces were fighting a gruesome war of ethnic genocide and close-quarter cold-blooded killing. Many of the soldiers, primarily from elite special forces, airborne brigades and crack infantry units, had already witnessed first-hand the muddles madness of the Balkans—they had walked through villages left empty by rape, ethnic cleansing and point-blank artillery barrages in UNPROFOR, IFOR and SFOR. Few had any doubts that their services would be needed once again in Kosovo.

But the impetus behind the annual exercise had little to do with the Balkans, though holding the exercises only 100 kilometers from a potential international flash-point was convenient. The framework of "Cooperative Best Effort" came as a logical successor to the previous Northern European Command Infantry Competition (NECIC) which was a squad-level exercise designed to assess the quality of the infantry within NATO's former Northern Region and to foster understanding and friendship among the soldiers of participating nations. There are many high-level PFP (Partnership for Peace) exercises for major headquarters and senior staffs, but relatively few that allow the ordinary soldier to get together with his counterparts from other NATO and partner nations. The

A Georgian trooper mans a checkpoint during "Cooperative Best Effort '98." Veterans of their own civil wars and guerrilla conflicts, the Georgians were impressive and seasoned. The soldier wears an indigenous-pattern Georgian-produced camouflage, and is armed with the light machine gun version of the Soviet-built RPK-74

The Azerbijanis impressed many of the soldiers participating in "Cooperative Best Effort '98" with their fierce combat skills. Here, at one of the ranges set up for the units participating in the exercise, Azerbijani troopers show their western counterparts what "marksmanship" truly is.

exercise, NATO officials hoped, would be less a stiff military maneuver, the kind of which NATO units usually participate in, but more importantly a "get-to-know-you" exchange where soldiers who wear the camouflage pattern of one nation can mingle and learn from counterparts in other countries. Best Effort enables participating squads to share experiences gained in peacekeeping operations over the years with the United Nations and NATO. CINCNORTHWEST's intention is to hold this exercise annually. Cooperative Best Effort 98 is the third such exercise—the first was held in the Czech Republic in September 96 and the second exercise held in Latvia in 1997. "Cooperative Best Effort '99" is scheduled for Quebec, Canada, in June 1999.

For a cross-continent and Trans-Atlantic comrades in arms endeavor, "Cooperative Best Effort '98" was certainly well-attended. The international assembly that arrived in Macedonia was impressive. They included:

- Germany: 571st Gebirgsjäger Mountain Battalion
- Canada: 22nd Royal Regiment
- Denmark: 4th Mechanized Company, Jutland Dragoons Regiment
- Spain: Pireneos Battalion, Aragon Mountain Brigade
- United States: 18th Infantry Regiment, 1st Infantry Division (Mechanized)
- France: 4th Company, 21st RIMa (*Regiment d'Infanterie de Marine*) Scorpions
- Greece: 601st Light Infantry Battalion, 71st Infantry Brigade
- Italy: Lagunari contingent
- Norway: 4th Company, His Majesty King's Guards
- The Netherlands: 13th Engineers Company, 13th Mechanized Brigade
- Portugal: special forces detachment
- United Kingdom: Prince of Wales Company, 1st Battalion Welsh Guards
- Turkey: 28th Mechanized Brigade (Ankara)
- Albania: 1st Civil Defense Regiment
- Austria: 4th Company, 7th Airmobile Regiment
- Azerbijan: a mechanized infantry unit
- Bulgaria: 3rd Infantry Battalion, 61st Mechanized Brigade
- Estonia: Public Security formation
- Republic of Georgia: a reconnaissance battalion
- Hungary: 88th Szolnok Rapid Reaction Battalion
- Lithuania: a special forces company
- Macedonia: 1st Battalion, 11th Motorized Brigade
- Moldavia: 1st Brigade, Balti Motorized Infantry
- Poland: NCO Airborne School Stefan Czarniecki
- Romania: 811th Infantry Battalion, 81st Mechanized Brigade
- Ukraine: a unit from the 95th Airmobile Brigade

The odd, and perhaps most successful aspect of "Cooperative Best Effort '98" was the fact that many of the participating nations were at odds with one another. In fact, NATO's thinking in creating this exercise

An Azerbijani soldier, legendary mountain warriors in their own right, peers through the sights of his AK-47 7.62mm assault rifle.

A Romanian soldier from the 811st Infantry Battalion, wearing their characteristic camouflage fatigues and red berets, insert 7.62mm rounds into banana-clip magazines for an afternoon of "fun and bang" on the range in Macedonia.

Turkish infantrymen, from the 28th Mechanized Brigade of Ankara (an elite unit that had seen its share of combat in eastern Turkey against Kurdish guerrillas), deploy for battle wearing the new Turkish camouflage uniform, as well as newly issued flak vests and helmets.

was to build a bridge, a combatant's brotherhood of sorts, that could extinguish national fears and prejudices; considering the fact that Romanians and Hungarians, Greeks and Turkish, and Macedonians and Albanians all worked together in a unified effort, was perhaps the endeavor's true success.

Although under the grouping of NATO's PFP initiative, most of the participating combatants realized that in the post Cold War Europe, especially in the Balkans, one "Prays for peace and prepare for war." At

the commencement of the exercise, participating soldiers did what infantrymen do whenever they get the opportunity—they raced for the range to try out new and exotic weapons. About 400 troops fired small arms from six countries, and then tried out clothing and equipment from all the countries taking part. British troopers fired French FAMAS rifles, Americans fired Polish PM-84 submachine guns, and Italians were able to test their skills with the "Super Galils" carried by the Estonians. Inevitably, and almost comically, there were some miscues and cultural clashes—especially between the haves and the have-nots! On the firing

A Turkish trooper pauses while clutching his Heckler and Koch G3 7.62mm assault rifle/M203 40mm grenade launcher system—a weapon that has proved incredibly useful in the counter-insurgency operations the brigade has waged in Kurdistan.

A Turkish NCO peers through his field glasses as his squad pauses during a long-range reconnaissance patrol deep into "guerrilla" territory during an "Cooperative Best Effort '98" exercise.

Excellent view of the new Turkish "elite unit" uniform and load-bearing gear.

An Estonian peace-keeper, manning a check-post, remains alert with his Israeli-produced "Super-Galil" 7.62mm sniper rifle.

Estonian security troopers, all armed with Israeli Glilon 5.56mm assault rifles, man a roadblock as a civilian couple passes through in the most convenient—and common—form of Macedonian mass transportation.

range, the commander was an American Special Forces major who, upon about to issue the green light to the men lined up to blast away, ordered that ear-protectors be worn. The Poles, not equipped with ear-protection, laughed, "My men are not young girls, but Polish soldiers!"

During Phase II of the exercise, several participating nations were tasked with conducting demonstrations and workshops applicable to peace-keeping operations. The Estonians, for example, were tasked with building searches; the Canadians with check-point procedures; the Macedonians with media relations; Greek forces were tasked with mine awareness; Dutch troops were responsible for escorting convoys; Polish troops were tasked with the identification and marking of unexploded ordinance; Romanian forces were issued with observation post procedures; Turkish troopers were the lucky souls asked to execute patrols and long-range reconnaissance; and, American forces were responsible for navigation and emergency medical evacuation. Making

Recipients of much Israeli military assistance and expertise, an Estonian sniper proudly displays his "Super-Galil" 7.62mm sniper rifle.

Phase II all the more challenging was the fact that torrential down pours flooded the training area turning it into a muddy mess.

The varying exercises, training scenarios and missions were all carried out with stark realism. Bulgarian soldiers showed onlookers how to search a building, at first approaching it cautiously, then flushing out "unfriendlies" with a lightning fast tactical assault. Dutch units on convoy patrol and Turkish forces slinking silently on patrol executed

A now all-too familiar feature of the Balkan landscape—a roadblock manned by international peace-keepers. Estonian troopers keep "non-invited" individuals clear of their sector courtesy of a roadside obstacle and some very capable trigger fingers.

Greek soldiers from the 601st Light Infantry Battalion of the 71st Infantry Brigade (a Rapid Deployment brigade), one of the truly unique and elite fighting formations of NATO's southern flank, fan out to the side of a Macedonian road to protect a convoy and BTR-80s of the Macedonian Army.

A Greek light infantryman peers through the sights of his G3 assault rifle during convoy-protection exercises.

Using a Macedonian BTR-80 for cover, a Greek light infantryman leaps out of his armored shelter during a mock assault on a peace-keeping convoy.

A young Greek soldier, clutching his G3, moves quickly to relieve a comrade walking point, during convoy protection exercises on a Macedonian rural road.

their tasks with equal seriousness.

The comparison of the different methods, the ability to observe another force's skills and shortcomings, were invaluable learning tools for the participating units. Yet Phase III, in which real-life peace-keeping scenarios were played out, was seen as the litmus test to see if the exercise would be a success. The various units role-played operations amid a civilian population, as well as scenarios in which they were attempting to carry out their day-to-day peace-keeping operations while under sniper and mortar fire. The Dutch engineers, in particular, impressed the international assembly, especially the French, when in one scenario they found themselves trapped under fire in a minefield.

On February 12, 1999, British troops were preparing their arms, equipment and vehicle for NATO deployment to Kosovo—similar preparations were carried out in the United States, Germany, Spain, France and Italy, as well as half a dozen other European nations. Marines, from the 24th Marine Expeditionary Unit based at Camp Lejeune, North Carolina, are already deployed near Kosovo as part of an amphibious ready group in the Mediterranean, were also set for deployment to the besieged war-zone; some 4,000 infantrymen and special forces personnel were also slated for deployment. The NATO mission inside the beleaguered province will be nearly impossible—separate two warring

parties who live side by side to one another and act as a buffer to protect a civilian population terrorized by hatred and victimized by wanton savagery. Few envy the men and women who will soon find themselves between a rock and an AK-47's barrel in Kosovo, but many of the peace-keepers, thanks to exercises like "Cooperative Best Effort" will be better equipped, better trained and far more intuitive to carry out their respective assignments, than ever before.

A Bulgarian soldier from the 3rd Battalion, 61st Mechanized Brigade, a special operations qualified unit that has made an international name for itself on peace-keeping assignments, gives the thumb's up following the successful entry of a suspected "hostile" building.

Peering through the sights of his G3, a Greek light infantryman from the 601st Battalion keeps his weapon trained on a "hostile" individual during "Cooperative Best Effort '98" convoy exercises.

22

Bulgarian peace-keepers check their gear prior to assaulting a suspected guerrilla structure during one of the more tactically energetic aspects of "Cooperative Best Effort '98."

Using a mirror and great caution, Bulgarian troopers assault a suspected guerrilla hide-out. Teamwork, as well as absolutely disciplined weapons control, is a prerequisite for safe and meticulous building entries and searches.

Responding to reports of sniper fire, Bulgarian mechanized troops race into action.

With the smoke of a distraction device yet to clear, a Bulgarian NCO directs his men to an additional location where guerrillas might be hiding and arms cached.

Stoic portrait of a Bulgarian NCO—directing his troops "under fire" and in a situation where they cannot respond with terminating and indiscriminate firepower.

Although in an exercise such as "Cooperative Best Effort '98" twenty-six different languages might prove a hindrance, the business-end of a 7.62mm assault rifle is a phrase that is universally understood.

Hungarian shock troops from the elite 88th Szolnok Rapid Reaction Battalion, a special forces capable heliborne raiding force, is briefed in the field prior to an operational deployment.

A Bulgarian sniper takes aim with his SVD Dragunov 7.62mm sniper rifle.

Hungarian operators from the 88th Szolnok Rapid Reaction Battalion examine a Canadian trooper's Minimi 5.56mm light machine gun.

Emerging as one of the dominant military powers of Central Europe, the 88th Szolnok Rapid Reaction Battalion has also emerged as one of Europe's true elite combat formations. Here, in a field in Macedonia, Hungarian troopers prepare to fan out during an "aggressive patrol."

Austrian paratroopers from the 7th Airborne Jägers test their skills on the range with a Romanian SVD.

Austrian para-hunters from the 7th Airborne Jägers focus on their target through the cross-hairs of a Romanian SVD 7.62mm sniper rifle.

Polish Airborne NCOs, the favorite among many of the participants to "Cooperative Best Effort '98" because of their unique esprit de corps, put on a demonstration simulating a riot against a United Nations observation post.

A Polish sniper unleashes a few 7.62mm rounds of fire from his SVD rifle.

Armed with the new Heckler and Koch G-36 assault rifle, a squad of German Gebirgsjäger mountain troops from the 571st Battalion move through a Macedonian field.

Polish snipers were also considered among the finest marksmen in the Warsaw Pact—and now that reputation has carried over to their new role as NATO's eastern-most bastion.

Spanish mountain trooper enjoys a chance to fire the coveted AK-47 7.62mm assault rifle.

Virtually invisible as a result of his impromptu camouflage, a Polish sniper takes a deep breath and slowly depresses on the trigger of his SVD 7.62mm assault rifle.

Welsh Guards sweep across an open field to recover food parcels air-dropped by C-130s. Note British Desert DPM and SA-80 5.56mm assault rifles carried.

A Welsh Guard NCO checks in with headquarters during a reshuffling of British objectives during the "Cooperative Best Effort" exercise.

Safeguarding food shipments, especially those dropped by air, can be extremely critical during a peace-keeping mission. Here, on a field turned into a food warehouse, British forces secure emergency parcels parachuted by NATO aircraft.

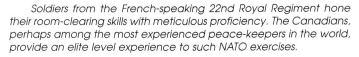

Soldiers from the French-speaking 22nd Royal Regiment hone their room-clearing skills with meticulous proficiency. The Canadians, perhaps among the most experienced peace-keepers in the world, provide an elite level experience to such NATO exercises.

Armed with his C-7 5.56mm assault rifle, a Canadian infantryman slowly and carefully searches and secures a suspected "unfriendly's" house.

Using the skill and expertise of an urban SWAT team, a Canadian 22nd Royal Regiment sergeant passes through the "all's clear" sign to his lieutenant outside of a dwelling being searched for arms and fugitives.

American soldiers from the 18th Infantry Regiment, 1st Infantry Division "Big Red One", carry a Zodiac inflatable and prepare for a river crossing.

American soldiers ford a river to ferry supplies and emergency medicine aid to a group of refugees in their sector of "Cooperative Best Effort '98."

Wearing their distinctive Woodland-pattern fatigues and carrying their M16A2 5.56mm assault rifle, American 18th Infantry Regiment troopers deploy from their Zodiac inflatable during a resupply sortie. Supplying a civilian population in a war-zone where roads are mined and ambushed, and guerrillas and hostile forces roam the countryside is dangerous business—and one that these American infantrymen prepare for with dire seriousness and professionalism.

The legendary "Big Red One!" An American lieutenant confers with headquarters as his radioman scans the countryside for any signs of hostile forces.

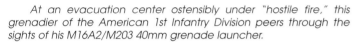

American troopers practice an evacuation scenario, after one of their own has been "taken down" by an enemy sniper.

At an evacuation center ostensibly under "hostile fire," this grenadier of the American 1st Infantry Division peers through the sights of his M16A2/M203 40mm grenade launcher.

The zigzag pattern of the Macedonian Air Force Mi-17, a helicopter seen here evacuating American infantrymen from a battlefield scenario, prepares to lift off for the race against the clock back to a field surgery unit.

American soldiers of the 18th Infantry Regiment prepare to embark on a day-long patrol of the Macedonian countryside during "Cooperative Best Effort '98."

A Special Forces instructor briefs a squad of American infantrymen during irregular warfare patrolling and ambushing exercises.

A French Marine gets his long-awaited chance to unleash thirty rounds of 7.62mm fire onto a target. The FAMAS, SA-80 or G-3 might be standard NATO-fare, but the legendary Kalashnikov is the coveted assault rifle that most American and Western European soldiers "want" to fire.

A Macedonian weapons instructor offers some of his expertise in the A-to-Z workings of an AK-47 assault rifle to a female French soldier.

30

Under the watchful gaze of a German instructor, a French Marine (Marsouin Porpoise) from 4^e Company/21^e RIMa (Scorpions) gets to test his skills on the Heckler and Koch G-36 assault rifle.

French Marines, elite veterans of Balkan peace-keeping missions, search a bombed-out building for booby-traps.

Close-up photograph of a typical "peace-keeping" sandbag firing position, manned by 4^e Company/21^e RIMa (Scorpions) Marines on a Macedonian road.

Reacting to a sniper attack, 4^e Company/21^e RIMa (Scorpions) Marines respond in kind with a furious barrage of 5.56mm fire from their FAMAS assault rifles.

A French sniper, armed with the GIAT FR-F2 7.62mm precision rifle, takes aim on an "unfriendly" during an attack on a peace-keeper's forward firing position. Note G2 sheet, with the faces of wanted war criminals, kept close at hand.

A 4^e Company/21^e RIMa (Scorpions) anti-tank gunner, armed with the LRAC 89mm rocket, sets aim on an "enemy" sniper position, awaiting the authorization from his commander to obliterate the sniper and his observer.

Under sniper fire, 4^e Company/21^e RIMa (Scorpions) Marines help a civilian and his donkey to leave the fields of fire.

Two Macedonian troopers from 1st Battalion, 11th Motorized "Scorpion" Brigade, observe an exercise during "Cooperative Best Effort '98."

A deafening bit of international weapons exchanges—on a field in Macedonia, soldiers from twenty-six nations exchange weapons and test their marksmanship skills.

A Macedonian BTR-80 races across a field open to snipers during convoy training with American infantrymen.

A Macedonian sniper, armed with a Yugoslavian-produced Zastava M76 7.92mm assault rifle, moves into firing position during a heated live-fire combat exercise.

The nerve-racking hell of crawling on one's gut, removing one's bayonet from its scabbard and poking the earth in search of the dreaded landmine.

Macedonian EOD specialists prepare to detonate a series of landmines uncovered in an agricultural field.

Officer Down Recovery Training
The Yonkers Police Department Emergency Service Unit (ESU)

Samuel M. Katz

Lieutenant Gary Hanley (left) and Police Officer John Rinciari, in front of an ESU truck at the city's Second Precinct.

It was one of those jobs with the potential for what cops refer to as *absolute chaos*—a shoot-out, a vehicular pursuit, and the potential for hostages being taken and innocent victims hurt or killed. An FBI team, part of an Asian-organized crime task force from the New York City field office, had come to Yonkers to execute a buy-and-bust sting with some heroin dealers and their Dominican bodyguards. The federal agents, most serving undercover, were unsure if the sellers were armed or not, but heroin dealers rarely came to a meet without some ballistic back-up. The FBI agents, too, decided to be ballistically prudent—especially since the buy was to transpire in the parking lot of a local shopping mall that, in the early afternoon hours, was to be crammed with shoppers. Tactical support would be needed and the Yonkers Police Department's Emergency Service Unit (ESU) got the call. The FBI team was well aware of the unit's reputation. The team, thirty-strong, was renown throughout Westchester County and the New York City area for its tactical skill, and that ability would be needed this sunny winter's day on a rooftop garage overlooking the New York State thruway.

The four ESU cops joining the FBI operation had suited up earlier at the city's Second Precinct half-a-mile away. Not knowing what to expect, they came ready for anything, armed with their MP5s and Benelli 12-gauge shotguns. At the tac-meeting, the ESU cops were glad they brought the firepower. The FBI agent-in-charge briefed the assembled group as to what would *hopefully* transpire that afternoon, though looking at the ESU cops, he was grateful to have made the phone call requesting assistance. "All we know is that the buyers are coming expecting the merchandise," the lead agent explained, "though every time we've dealt with these characters, they've had a support crew of two Dominicans from northern Manhattan, who have served as lookouts. In fact, their guys have routinely gone on reconnaissance runs and stake-outs of their own of the parking lots where we've had our meets." As the agents and Yonkers cops listened to the briefing, one of the ESU cops jotted down the license plate

number of the Dominicans' vehicle on his right hand with a marker. He realized that if the vehicle were to be found—ESU would be responsible with the takedown. "I don't know if the Dominicans are heavily armed," the FBI supervisor concluded, "but I want to be ready just in case."

As the FBI agents headed toward their vehicles to slip into their Kevlar vests and FBI wind-breakers, Lieutenant Gary Hanley, the ESU commanding officer, simulated a car take-down in case the suspect vehicle was spotted. Lieutenant Hanley, a nationally-recognized tactical trainer, always makes sure that smallest of details in any job are never taken for granted. Sloppiness can lead to tragedy in a profession where automatic weapons are deployed and split-second judgment are as crucial a tool as one's ballistic vest. Using a patrol car as the targeted vehicle, Lieutenant Hanley went through the motions of approaching the stopped car, as he was joined by one officer in approaching the driver side, while the two other officers moved in on the passenger side. In a well-choreographed scene, practiced a hundred times before both in training and on the streets, the officers simulated the vehicle stop and the safe and secure removal of the occupants from the car. Two run-throughs were carried out before the ESU cops checked their Kevlar helmets and tactical vests, and played that awful anxious game cops are all experts at—the art of "hurry up and wait." Sitting in their two response cars, the ESU officers monitored the radio and clutched their weapons. Finally, after nearly an hour of laying low in the lot, the magic words—"car in sight" were heard over the secure frequency. Gunning their engines, the ESU response team raced toward the arrest, hoping to reach the perpetrator's back-up car before they could attempt to interfere with the FBI operation. The FBI undercover agent riding with Lieutenant Hanley readied his door for the burst out of the car, but the FBI observation team on the roof of the mall lost sight of the targeted vehicle that had probably slipped back on the thruway sensing a trap. As nervous shoppers looked on, unmarked cars and Yonkers Police Caprices raced about the open-air lot in search of the

Prior to a tac-meeting with FBI agents, the four-man ESU team suits up for action.

The Yonkers ESU truck.

car, a gold Honda, but it wasn't found. About 100 yards away, at the far end of the main entrance to the mall, a dozen FBI agents had rushed the heroin buyer, now wearing a brand new set of cuffs, the arrested individual angrily scanned the lot for his hired guns. ESU's firepower wasn't needed this blustery winter's day, but the back up was much appreciated.

With a population of over 200,000, the City of Yonkers would be considered a metropolis in many states, though when compared to New York City, its neighbor to the south, many in the state consider it to be the true definition of suburbia. Situated in Westchester County, Yonkers is a middle-class town with banks on the mighty Hudson River, tree-lined streets, affluent homes, and a growing population encompassing virtually every socio-economic demographic group imaginable. If ever there was a melting pot and a mosaic of races, cultures and bank accounts blended into one community, Yonkers is it. Yet because it borders New York City, sharing a frontier with four precincts in the Bronx, and virtually all of Westchester County's main thoroughfares, the Yonkers Police Department is faced with an ever-changing, highly mobile crime problem. Yet Yonkers is a far cry from being a footnote with a view of the Manhattan skyline. It is the fourth largest city in the state, and it has all the problems of a big city, from housing projects to prostitution, of its neighbor to the south together with the look and mind-set of a small-town.

The Yonkers Police Department is a fair-sized force consisting of 560 officers. The department is organized into three bureaus—the Investigation Services Bureau, the Support Services Bureau, and the Field Services Bureau. The Investigation Services Bureau consists of a Special Investigations Division and a Detective Division, and the Support

Services Bureau consists of Administrative Services Division, the Courts and Detention Division and the Training Division. The Field Services Bureau, commanded by Deputy Chief Joseph Kostik, consists of the department's patrol force divided into four precincts. The First Precinct covers the northeast quadrant of the city, responsible for nearly seven square miles of the city; the Second Precinct covers the southeast quadrant of the city, consisting of both major residential and commercial areas, and borders the Bronx to the south and Mount Vernon to the east; the Third Precinct covers the southwest quadrant of the city, from the Bronx to the south, and the Hudson River to the west; and, the Fourth Precinct encompasses the northwest quadrant of the city.

The Field Services Bureau also commands the department's Special Operations Division, or SOD, which includes the Traffic Enforcement Unit, K-9, and, until it was recently decentralized, one of the elite tactical units in New York State, the Emergency Service Unit; today, ESU operates three trucks out of three patrol precincts. Like its sister unit in New York City, Yonkers' ESU is designed as a multi-talented force that can handle any—and all—emergencies conceivable within the precincts of the city, and within the boundaries of the county. The unit has a dual tactical and rescue task, and all officers are trained EMTs. Yonkers ESU handles road-wrecks and pin-jobs, animal jobs, EDPs, jumpers, ice and water rescues and, of course, tactical back up and support to the patrol force. With twenty-eight officers and two lieutenants, the unit is large enough to meet its daunting workload, yet small enough to enjoy an esprit de corps and professional ethic identifiable with some of the most renowned tactical teams in the country.

Yonkers ESU began in the mid-1930s as a jack-of-all trades unit that could address emergencies patrol cars simply were untrained and ill-

Atop a shopping mall parking lot, Lieutenant Hanley runs through the choreography of a vehicle take-down with his men.

The FBI take-down in Yonkers.

During officer recovery training, Lieutenant Hanley (center) explains the purpose and importance of the day's training.

equipped to handle. That tradition of serving as back up for the officers on patrol continues to this day, though the tactical responsibility has increased significantly since the days the unit was formed. The unit's primary task is to patrols the city's sectors in four trucks, a cabin of emergency and tactical gear loaded on a 4x4 pickup, that store both the rescue equipment. On patrol, the unit has encountered the 360° gamut of jobs—ranging from chasing deer and bears through the city streets with tranquilizer guns, to talking down jumpers from housing project ledges and church steeples, to extracting trapped motorists from the remnants of their twisted vehicles. On patrol anything and everything can and has happened—from barricaded criminals holding hostages, to EDPs prancing on the outer ledge of a twenty-story housing project. There is no ordinary day in the unit, no boredom or settling into the routine of the mundane.

One unique ESU job occurred in the summer of 1996, when quick thinking and guts were all that stood between a miraculous rescue or a tragedy that would haunt the cops for years. On one sunny morning, on a tree-lined street, in an affluent neighborhood in the city, a nanny-gone-berserk had taken her charge, a six-month-old baby, hostage. The nanny wasn't asking for ransom, or that any demands be met. She was simply squeezing the child by the neck with psychotic fervor, as she dangled it out the window. The responding ESU officers realized that this was no ordinary EDP, and the time for negotiations or non-lethal means of containment had long since passed. Officer John Rinciari, a seven-year veteran of the unit and one of its instructors with over twenty years on the job, together with his partner, Officer Frank Campana, quickly entered the house, while another ESU tandem of Officer Wilson Gonzalez and Jim Pennachio made entrance through a garage door, to distract the woman while the other officers attempted the grab. The ESU cops raced

Officer Patti-Anne Pavacic, ESU's sole female officer, listens in as Lieutenant Hanley briefs the training cadre.

throughout the house, left in shambles by the nanny's deranged outburst, and managed to pounce on her while the baby was freed and rushed outside to an awaiting ambulance. The baby was lucky to have suffered only minor cuts and bruises. It took six ESU officers to eventually subdue and restrain the tiny woman.

The unit is a busy one for a force of its size. In 1997, it responded to over 1,500 aided requests; over 400 EDP jobs, over 400 animal control requests, nearly 1,000 motor-vehicle accidents, over fifty public demonstrations, 150 rescues (elevator, water emergencies, HAZMAT, and ice rescues); and, nearly 300 tactical situations, ranging from high-risk warrants, to barricaded perpetrators, to assisting patrol and narcotics units in the arrests of armed suspects. In fact, the unit's true distinction is its tactical skill and dedication to training. Many of the officers have

The Yonkers ESU Peace-Keeper.

Suited up and armed with an M-16 5.56mm assault rifle, an ESU officer awaits the call to action inside the passenger seat of the Peace-Keeper.

Officer John Rinciari, center, simulating a pinned down officer, is approached by a rescue team deploying from the Peace-Keeper and then brought into safety.

An ESU officer readies his MP5 from the bin of his ESU truck, prior to an early morning high-risk drug warrant near Yonkers Raceway.

received training from the FBI Hostage Rescue Team (HRT) and the National Tactical Officers Association (NTOA). ESU commander Lieutenant Hanley has traveled the country—and the world—visiting various tactical and emergency response units and has brought back many of the tactics and professional ethics to his unit. Yonkers ESU, in fact, trains most of the tactical teams in Westchester County. In 1993, in fact, when the New York City Housing Police (now merged with the NYPD) created its own Emergency Rescue Unit (ERU), it was Yonkers ESU that provided them with special weapons and tactics instruction. Although the Housing Police has now merged with the NYPD, and Housing Rescue has merged with the NYPD's Emergency Service Unit, many housing ERU veterans recall their training in Yonkers with great fondness and incredible gratitude. "The unit is a credit to the department and the City of Yonkers," reflects a former housing rescue cop now serving in one of the busier NYPD Emergency Service trucks, "and its refreshing that when you are the new kid on the block, one of the state's elite tactical units, if not the best in the area, let's you play in their sandbox and doesn't, in the process, kick sand in your face." The training that Yonkers ESU provided the newly formed housing team was all-inclusive, and designed to prepare them to meet any challenge they might encounter while responding to emergencies in one of the toughest beats in America. "The knowledge, assistance and level of professionalism in Yonkers ESU is unsurpassed, the Housing Rescue officer recalls, "for a unit that size, they demand a work ethic and attention to detail the likes of which I have yet to see in most police teams. They perfect tried and true methods of operation, though aren't afraid to go against the traditional rule of thumb and try something new. You will not find a closer-knit group of cops who love what they do anywhere else in law enforcement."

Yonkers ESU has also, on countless occasions, left the city confines to assist neighboring units and departments on everything from building searches to high-risk bank stake-outs with the FBI. Because of the make-up of Westchester County, where towns interlock with one another and

car-chases and other criminal matters often cross from one jurisdiction to another in the blink of an eye, Yonkers ESU has been called out on hundreds of occasions to provide tactical back-up to a half dozen other units and departments in the area. Yonkers K-9, which always deploys with ESU back-up, conducts many of the perp and building searches in neighboring Mount Vernon, they have traveled to the eastern stretches of the county to serve as tactical advisors to a small department faced with a barricaded gunman and no tactical unit to deploy. Yonkers ESU has traveled as far as the Connecticut border in working with the FBI to stop a gang of heavily-armed bank robbers hitting branches from Rye to Greenwich. Yonkers ESU also enjoys a close-knit working relationship with federal law enforcement entities, such as the FBI, the DEA and ATF. Interestingly enough, many "alleged" organized crime figures, including the recently arrested John Gotti Jr., reside in Yonkers and, as a result, federal investigations in the city's confines are aggressive and constant.

Inter-department cooperation is viewed as a matter of great importance to the officers in Yonkers ESU, especially on large-jobs where the units and resources of one department's tactical team might be insufficient to deal with a developing crisis. One such instance occurred in the small-town of Eastchester, just over the Bronx border, in central Westchester County. On Thursday, March 21, 1996, Richard Sacchi, described as a loner and long known in the town as an EDP, called in a complaint to 911 and then waited by his window, armed with a high-powered rifle, as the patrol car pulled up in front of his house. Eastchester Police Officer Michael Frey, a cop who left work in the New York City Transit Police for a safer type of police work away from the big city, was shot in the head as he was about to get out of his car, and then shot

Police Officer John Rinciari peers through the sights of his M-16 in the Peace-Keeper's cupola, as fellow officers undertake the rescue of a pinned-down officer.

While one officer covers their movements through the firing port of the Peace-Keeper's rear door, the two-man stretcher team races out to the wounded officer, and then back with the safely recovered victim.

Deploying their ballistic body bunkers from the rear of the Peace-Keeper, an ESU fire-team takes aim, while the officer down is placed inside a stretcher.

multiple times for good measure. Frey's partner, Officer Richard Morrissey, was grazed by a bullet though pinned down by sustained fire behind the police car. As Eastchester cops raced to the scene, responding to a job the likes of which they had never thought could happen in their picturesque community, Sacchi barricaded himself inside this house with his grandmother, taunting responding cops with fusillades of gunfire from several weapons of varying caliber. The fifty officers of the Eastchester Police Department were ill equipped and outgunned to cope with a barricaded psycho armed with scoped weapons. Their sleepy town had nice homes and manicured lawns—not gun battles with automatic weapons. Eastchester Police Chief James Maher summoned immediate assistance from neighboring New Rochelle, and their police chief, a former commander of NYPD's Emergency Service Unit, placed an urgent request for tactical assistance from New York City.

Shortly after Frey was murdered, NYPD ESU officers from the Bronx and Queens arrived on the scene. A Peace-Keeper armored car and an M75 ERV (Emergency Rescue Vehicle) were brought up to Eastchester, as was a robot, the R.M.I. (remote mobile investigator), and even the unit's counter-sniper team. Lieutenant Hugh McGowan and the NYPD's nationally esteemed Hostage-Negotiations Team also headed north to Eastchester. After rescuing Officer Morrissey and removing the lifeless body of Officer Frey from the patrol car, ESU engaged in a precarious fourteen-hour attempt to negotiate Sacchi's surrender. At around 3:30 A.M. the following morning, after all reasonable attempts to reach Sacchi came up fruitless, ESU went in. At first, the robot went in. Equipped with a mounted video camera, the robot allowed the E-cops to gain a bird's-eye of a house. After the robot, NYPD K-9 units went in, followed by a cautious advance of ESU cops, making their covert entry. At 5:00 A.M., after fourteen hours of terror, the siege at Eastchester had ended. Inside the house, cops found the gunmen dead from a self-inflicted gunshot wound, as well as the body of his eighty-eight-year-old grandmother. Cops also found a .22 caliber rifle, a 12-gauge shotgun, and a World War Two vintage 30.06 Garand rifle.

Eastchester was as a wake-up call to law enforcement officials in Westchester County—it was a Pearl Harbor of sorts, a point of no return, where local units and departments would need to find the means to call upon each other's services, talents and equipment in a timely and reasonable manner should a job develop that one department, for whatever reason, simply could not handle by itself. Eastchester, for example, was only three-tenth of a mile from the Yonkers city lines, yet Yonkers ESU, also equipped with Peace-Keeper armored cars, was never summoned to the job. If there is one constant in police work, especially in tactical response units, it is that by preparing for the absolute worst scenario possible, a team guarantees being ready for what ever comes down the road. Yonkers ESU realized that there might very well be future Eastchesters either in their town, or in their neighboring communities, and that it was important for them to be adequately trained to respond to an officer down situation of their own.

On one rainy and frigid winter's morning, a group of ESU officers assembled in the parking lot of a factory complex to conduct a grueling day's instruction on evacuating a wounded officer with a Peace-Keeper armored car. The training was important and heart-felt to many of the

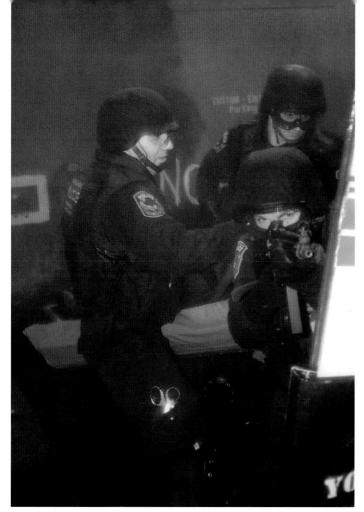

While Officer Patti-Anne Pavacic peers through the sights of her MP5, the stretcher team safely returns to the rear-entrance of the Peace-Keeper.

Before racing away from the embattled fire-zone, ESU deploys a smoke cover to disguise its withdrawal back to safety.

officers, most of who had attended the Frey funeral and had spoken to the NYPD emergency service officers who handled the difficult job in such a professional manner. The officers attending the hands-on training seminar came on their own time on their day off. "It's a reflection of the type of guys that Yonkers has in its unit," claims an NYPD ESU officer, "that they would go the extra mile to make their job a safer one, and their city a safer place."

The scenario of the training was simple—an officer or civilian is pinned down under heavy gunfire and its ESU's job, with the Peace-Keeper serving as both an armored personnel carrier and mobile ballistic shield, to safely secure his evacuation. The fact that the training was being conducted in the rear parking lot of a Civil War-era factory complex was an added bonus of realism and effect. Unlike the grassy-stretches of a training ground, the complex of windows and potential sniper perches allowed the participating officers to absorb the terrifying reality of coming up against a gunmen fortified in an urban setting. The training was meant to simulate an actual environment in which the officers might one day find themselves—not the hypothetical elements of "imagine what if." Operating the cumbersome Peace-Keeper in the narrow confines of a crowded parking lot added an additional sense of reality to the training. After all, what happens when you need to respond to a pinned down civilian or fellow officer in an area in which it is difficult to maneuver your armored protection? Both Lieutenant Hanley and Lieutenant Joe Barca, ESU's two supervisors, in designing the day's training, had but one objective in mind—make sure Yonkers ESU was ready when a frantic call for help would summon them into action.

The first scenario of the day involved a civilian pinned down and wounded in a corner of the square, dangerously exposed to the gunman's sights. The Peace-Keeper, parked 100 yards away, negotiated the narrow traffic lanes toward the victim, attempting to maneuver the hulking

vehicle amid rows of parked cars and other obstacles. The driving was difficult—it might have been hellatious under dedicated gunfire. Once the Peace-Keeper actually reached the victim, however, the true—and very—dangerous work of safe recovery commenced. Officers had to deploy from the rear of the Peace-Keeper, they needed to deploy officers to cover potential threats with their MP5s and M-16 assault rifles, and they needed to deploy an evacuation team to carry the Reeves stretcher to the victim, properly fasten him to the stretcher, and then return him to the safety of the armored car. The wet and windy conditions only added to the difficulty of the exercise.

For officers used to driving a Chevy Caprice, or even the ESU truck, negotiating the narrow spaces with the Peace-Keeper is difficult work. Maneuvering the vehicle toward the wounded civilian is even harder, and in position where the officers can exit the vehicle safely is most difficult. Lieutenant Barca and Hanley jot down mental notes, as they observe the Peace-Keeper come to a stop, its doors wing open and the officers emerge. First, the bunker-team sets up protective cover, as two officers peer through the sights of their MP5s and M-16s at the surrounding windows and rooftops. Another two officers emerge with the bright-red Reeves stretcher and rush to the victim. Evacuation is more important at this point than immediate medical care, and the patient is strapped into the stretcher and carefully inserted into the belly of the armored car. Once he is securely inside, the bunker team slowly enters the Peace-Keeper, making sure that their shields are raised beyond the rear-doors of the vehicle. Once the officers are all inside, the shield is discarded on the pavement and the Peace-Keeper speeds off to a safe location where the victim can receive medical attention.

Following each run-through, both Lieutenants Hanley and Barca point out observations and items they'd like to see corrected, and Officer John Rinciari, provides some comments of his own, reflecting on his experiences on the job, and from observing some of the elite tactical teams in the country and the world in action. The exercises aren't designed to show the cops that they are doing something wrong, but rather they are meant to strike their minds with the thought process that when bullets are actually flying, mistakes in basic tactics can get people killed.

A second-scenario involves an incident much like the killing at Eastchester. Officer John Rinciari plays the role of a cop pinned down by gunfire. Trapped by his patrol car, the responding Peace-Keeper must pull to within several yards of the besieged officer and then deploy a bunker team to pull him to safety. As the Peace-Keeper moves toward the patrol car, an officer emerges through the vehicle's turret to aim his M-16 through the protected cupola. The Peace-Keeper stops and the officers emerge. In a slow and well-choreographed advance, the bunker team gingerly slinks back toward the officer. Raising their shields, the team

During building entry training, ESU officers race in through an open door with weapons at the ready.

During tubular assault training on a commuter train, Police Officer John Rinciari races through the car in search of hostage-takers.

reaches the pinned-down officer and instructs him to grab on to their tac vest and follow them toward the Peace-Keeper. Officer Rinciari, simulating an officer who has been involved in a shoot-out, is still holding his Glock as he is directed into the rear of the armored car. "You didn't instruct the pinned down cop to holster his weapon," Lieutenant Hanley points out, "if he was wounded and possibly squeezes the trigger once inside the Peace-Keeper the results would have been messy. Remember, inside the locked contraption, a round that is discharged will continue to bounce around until it hits something soft." The point for tactical safety is well taken by the officers. The scenario is replayed, and replayed again, until Lieutenants Hanley and Barca feel that the lessons have been learned and mistakes corrected. "You have to vocalize your commands to the officer," Lieutenant Barca points out, "you need to let him know that you are the one's who'll direct his evacuation. He's been in a shoot-out and he might be wounded or dazed by the fact that his partner has been hurt or killed. He might not want to surrender his gun. You have to take control and be in charge!"

The training lasts for nearly eight hours and concludes with an officer recovery exercise in which smoke devices are deployed for cover, and a building entry for good measure. Every scenario is videotaped and photographed, so that the training can be analyzed and critiqued at a later date. Back at work, after the training concluded, several officers approached Lieutenants Hanley and Barca to tell them that *they too* would gladly give up a day off in order to participate in additional tactical instruction. "It's a great reflection on the officers in the unit," Lieutenant Hanley says with pride, "that they are always willing to go the extra mile." It's that esprit de corps, in fact, that has come to characterize Yonkers ESU. "I look forward to going to work every day," says Officer Rinciari, "it's a privilege to be in ESU and to serve the cops and people of the city!"

Awaiting the order to assault a "hijacked commuter train" during tubular assault exercises, Police Officer Frank Campana stands at the ready.

Using the Peace-Keeper as cover, an ESU assault element moves into firing position.

Yonkers ESU officer Frank Campana moves about a commuter rail car crammed with New York Metropolitan area tactical officers during tubular assault exercises in Upstate New York.

Another day shift has passed for Yonkers ESU, with the routine of patrol, for once at least, has ended without bizarre incident. Back at the ESU office at police headquarters, Lieutenants Hanley and Barca prepare the final groundwork for a warrant that the unit will be serving for narcotics the following morning. The targeted drug den, located on a residential block, is a twenty-four-hour-a-day operation, but it's decided to go in just after dawn when the midnight crew will probably be dozing off in front of the TV. Nothing is left for chance, and no detail is too small to be ignored. It's part of the ethic that the unit prides itself with. The following morning, just after 4:00 A.M., ten weary-eyed ESU cops head to headquarters for the tac meeting. The briefing is lengthy and highly detailed. Lieutenants Hanley and Barca have brought maps and diagrams of the location to the meeting, and each aspect of the team's arrival, entry and deployment inside the house is elaborated in great detail. Before the team heads toward the unmarked van that will ferry them to their location, they go through a brief dry run of the entry and what each officer's task will be. The dry run is flawless, as is the actual warrant. Successful entry is made courtesy of a battering ram, and the drug dealers and the evidence that will later be used against them in a court of law are secured and seized in a dynamic, and picture-perfect, entry. The warrant has gone well, and, with the smoke of the diversionary devices still billowing throughout the apartment, the two lieutenants debrief the officers as to their observations on operation.

A twenty-year veteran with the Los Angeles Police Department's SWAT Platoon, who had trained with the unit, considers the cops in Yonkers ESU to be among the most dedicated and enthusiastic he has ever seen. Such accolades, coming from a member of perhaps the finest municipal police tactical team in the world, is as powerful a compliment as can be earned in the tactical community. Yet on the streets of the city and throughout Westchester County, Yonkers ESU has displayed their dedication and enthusiasm in their everyday and diverse tasks on patrol, and when they serve as the department's—and the county's—premier tactical back-up force.

ESU training officer John Rinciari peers through the sights of his Glock 9mm during a tense stand-off in Yonkers.

Those tense first few moments through the door —Yonkers ESU officers hone their room entry skills.

The Elite of The Pacific Northwest
The Portland Police Bureau
Special Emergency Reaction Team

Samuel M. Katz

Portland SERT officers remove an "officer down" during recovery training north of Portland. (Courtesy: Joe Savage/Portland PB-SERT)

Subdued Portland Police Bureau

Portland Police Bureau SERT patch

Portland Police Bureau

It was afternoon in a bustling section of downtown Portland when, outside the KOIN Tower, a monolith in the Portland, Oregon, the day-to-day routine as business as usual was interrupted by the crackling sound of automatic gun fire and frantic calls to 911. James Henry Rinckner, a disgruntled employee, had entered the KOIN in a basement, and armed with a SKS rifle, a shotgun, and a handgun, was out to initiate a bloodbath. In the building's basement, he shot the first person he saw. As he raced toward the elevators, his SKS jammed though he resorted to his handgun and 12-gauge shotgun, firing rounds into the air. The smoke and flying dust triggered the elevators emergency alarms, and the elevators locked down. Panicking, Rinckner grabbed hostages and pushed them inside to a nearby Charles Schwab Investment Co. office.

Arriving officers were met with a deluge of information pertaining to the gunman turned hostage-taker. Taking up perimeter positions around

the office and dangerously close to Rinckner, though they immediately realized that this job was beyond the capacity of the training and their department issue Glocks. The patrol supervisor, hunkered down by his Chevy Caprice, looked at one of his sergeants and said, "Page SERT forthwith!"

In Portland, hostages meant an immediate police response and it meant the specialized skills and talents of the SERT- the Portland Police Bureau's elite Special Emergency Reaction Team.

SERT officers racing to the scene found the street-corner in chaos. Sniper positions were quickly established and officers began looking through intelligence material at their disposal as they began to formulate a tactical rescue plan. The situation was, indeed, grim and it was quickly deteriorating. Rinckner began ordering his hostages to call their loved

42

The Juvenile Justice Center of Multnomah County, Portland, Oregon. (Courtesy: Joe Savage/Portland PB-SERT)

SERT officers reach the besieged Juvenile Justice Center and gear up as they await a full briefing and a discussion of their tactical plan. (Courtesy: Joe Savage/Portland PB-SERT)

ones and say goodbye. As helicopters buzzed overhead, many feared the worst. The Hostage-Negotiating Team began to work on Rinckner, the sight of the officers peering through the sights of the MP5 submachine guns began to sink in. He realized he was in a lose-lose situation and his only possible recourse was to surrender.

As local newscasters reported live on TV from the beseiged area of downtown Portland, predicting a massacre, James Henry Rinckner sent his hostages out as he came out with his hands held high to the commands of the SERT commander. Once again SERT had saved the day.

It has been said that there stands a thin blue line of law enforcement between today's criminal element—the new form and breed of terrorism that has gripped it all—and the sheer fabric of law abiding society, but most police officers, by the very nature of their work, can only respond after the fact, to pick up the pieces and lay a yellow body bag over the latest crime scene. Yet in every military force or police unit, there is a small core of elite men and women who are tasked with the most dangerous, most desperate jobs meant to diffuse a potentially explosive situation, and provide a degree of professionalism, firepower and on-scene wisdom that will respond in kind when deadly force and tactical precision are the sole answers. These units are on-call in the course of their day-to-day activities, awaiting that call on the radio, the beeping rings on their pagers; as their skills are so unique and their numbers so small when compared to the rest of the forces or units they serve, that they in essence become on-call twenty-four hours a day. Most American municipal police forces have fostered and nourished such a unit to deal

with hostages, high-risk criminal and potential terrorist attacks in their cities. In Portland, that task falls to the Police Bureau's elite Special Emergency Reaction Team (or "SERT"). When the street officer in the Portland, Oregon's Police Bureau calls for help, it is the Special Emergency Reaction Team that responds. It is a twenty-man force of volunteers that because of the nature of their work, intensity of their tactical training and weapon's proficiency, make them truly a unique and celebrated force not only in American circles, but also around the world.

The Portland's SERT was created in 1975 within the department's elite intelligence unit. A six man team consisting of five officers and one sergeant comprised the original group. Besides regular intelligence duties these officers would respond to crisis or tactical situations beyond the scope or logistical abilities of street officers in the Uniform Division with their personal equipment considerations based on a military style model. Team members were armed with revolvers as personal sidearm and shoulder weapons were 12-gauge shotguns or Armalite AR-18 assault rifles. Sniper weapons available was whatever bolt action rifle that became available through confiscation in the property room.

SERT's initial team structure, operational philosophy, member selection and physical assessment processes were patterned after the LAPD SWAT Platoon after early SERT personnel attended an LAPD SWAT training class. In 1985 SERT members attended their first Los Angeles County Sheriff's Department Special Weapons Team basic special weapons and tactics school. SERT members left the school with a new understanding involving the principles and concepts of slow/covert

In a combined operation exemplifying inter-agency cooperation, Multnomah County CERT officers and Portland SERT operators prepare their inevitable assault. (Courtesy: Joe Savage/Portland PB-SERT)

Under the watchful gaze of CERT officers, Portland SERT operators remove bars and obstacles from facility windows as they embark on their retaking of the Juvenile Justice Center of Multnomah County. (Courtesy: Joe Savage/Portland PB-SERT)

As SERT officers maintain close cover with their 12-gauge shotguns, hardened windows are extracted in preparation of gas agents into the jail. (Courtesy: Joe Savage/Portland PB-SERT)

Under full tactical cover, SERT team officers deploy CS gas inside the besieged jail. (Courtesy: Joe Savage/Portland PB-SERT)

clears. New SERT members continue to attend that school whenever possible as it a Mecca of learning to develop proper attitudes about the ever-changing tactics and techniques required of municipal police tactical teams.

During this period a formal selection process for new members was implemented which utilized Bureau wide postings of orders from the Personnel Division announcing openings in the unit. Applicants for the team completed an arduous physical assessment as well as a formal oral board interview. In concert with these activities, an extensive in-house background investigation was completed on each applicant developing a summary of his performance as a police officer. That system of selection is continued today with tremendous success.

SERT currently consists of twenty officers. One sergeant and one officer serve full time with administrative and training issues and are also active members of the team. The remaining sergeant and officers work in other bureau patrol assignments, including precinct patrol, gang enforcement, and narcotics. Each SERT officer is issued a pager and is on twenty-four hour emergency call up unless excused for other commitments.

The team consists of two elements. One sergeant and eight officers comprise the "Assault Element" and one sergeant and ten members make up the "Inner Perimeter Element." The Assault Element is responsible for planning and executing entry into hostile environs for hostage rescue, high risk warrant service and armed, barricaded suspects. The Inner

Perimeter Element has as its duties the establishment of secure containment around a target location where the situation is occurring. Counter sniper/observer teams are deployed to use their particularly accurate skills to save lives and act as crucial intelligence gatherers to relay information to the Assault Element who will be busy planning rescue alternatives. In the event of a barricaded suspect the IP team will plan the delivery of tear-gas into the location to force the suspect out to an arrest team or inevitable showdown.

One recent "incident" occurred in 1997 when a young man raced into a bank, armed with a .357 Magnum, demanding cash. He held a

Another inmate is taken from the facility by Multnomah County CERT officers under the supervision of Portland SERT officers. (Courtesy: Joe Savage/Portland PB-SERT)

As Portland SERT officers cover, Multnomah County CERT officers remove an inmate from the facility. (Courtesy: Joe Savage/Portland PB-SERT)

Portland SERT teams support a U.S. Secret Service CAT team during a presidential visit to Oregon. (Courtesy: Joe Savage/Portland PB-SERT)

Two SERT officers man a defensive post outside a hotel in downtown Portland where President Clinton addressed a political gathering. (Courtesy: Joe Savage/Portland PB-SERT)

female teller at gunpoint and ordered the staff into a vault where he began to empty its contents. One of the tellers, though, managed to trip a silent alarm and patrol units raced to the scene; SERT officers were immediately summoned. SERT counter-snipers immediately raced to nearby windows and ledges to gain optimum visual coverage, while uniform patrolmen and SERT officers manned a secure perimeter. Over the course of time, negotiations commenced and continued, yet the robber continued to hold the two hostages, including a pregnant female. The robber was beginning to display erratic behavior and signs of violence. When negotiators balked at one of the more bizarre demands, the robber fired a shot inside the bank. Fearing that a hostage had been killed, SERT officers were issued with a clear order—if the snipers get a clear shot at the perpetrator, they have the green light to take the subject out.

SERT officers attempted to flush the robber out with a ruse, yet when he emerged from the bank to accept a note, the robber duck *just as* a sniper's round was fired; the round grazed the gunman and hit a counter. Realizing that a dynamic end to the ordeal was required, SERT officers lobbed several diversionary devices into the bank and stormed the location with MP5s in hand. The robber raised his weapon at the oncoming officers, prompting an eighteen-round fusillade that terminated the incident—and the robber—in a furious barrage of fire.

At every emergency occurrence SERT has a variety of Command and Support Staff available. The SERT Commander, a lieutenant, acts as a liaison between the team and the Incident Commander at the scene. The Incident Commander, depending on which Precinct the situation occurs in can be a different person form call to call. Having the same SERT Commander who is knowledgeable about the team's capabilities is vital for a successful resolution of any crisis.

In the event that SERT is called to a "job" (the now universal police term for an incident) the hostage negotiators, a group of specially trained detectives respond to the scene and attempt to talk to the suspect in an effort to resolve the situation peacefully. The Portland Police Bureau's Explosive Disposal Unit (EDU) is also made available for counter-terrorist work. The EDU is responsible for making the charges that SERT will use for explosive entry whether it's a full scale door or wall entry or a smaller charge for blowing a lock or hinges. EDU also has a robot that has many tactical uses. Not only does EDU uses the robot for bomb manipulation and destruction but the tracked vehicle's claws and camera work very well in delivering gas and looking into dangerous places without bodily risk.

One of the many support units that SERT has access to is one deemed most important. A pool of 12 Fire/Medics from the Portland Fire Bureau is readily available at each emergency occurrence as well as high risk warrants. Also on the same pager system these highly trained EMT's have spent considerable time training with SERT members and are

familiar with the operations and weapons used by SERT. Four of them will respond to assist each time the pager goes off.

It has been said that "as you train, so will you fight" and the SERT's hallmark is detailed training, planning and preparation—before entering a structure, officers usually know every door, every room and every light switch. Often, the SERT rehearses every step of their planned tactical move on a chalked diagram on the floor.

Like a special forces military unit, weapons proficiency is stressed in the SERT. From the basics of stance, sight picture, and trigger control to the more advanced stages of peel shooting hostage/suspect targets on the move, SERT spends many hours a month on weapons training. The Assault Element uses as their primary weapon the Heckler and Koch MP5A2, A3, and SD models mounted with Surefire fore stock tactical lights; this 9mm automatic sub gun is perfect for maneuvering in all types of situations. All SERT members carry—as a back up weapon—the Glock 17 9mm automatic, many equipped with the Surefire tactical light. Counter Snipers use the Remington Model 700 .308 caliber heavy barrel mounted with a Leopold 3.5 x 10 scope. Sniper Observers and other Inner Perimeter members carry a variety of assault rifles which include the M-16 and CAR-15 5.56mm assault rifles, or the Heckler and Koch 91 and 93 models. Most assault rifles are mounted with Pro Point illuminated dot scopes and lighting systems. A Litton Starlight scope is readily available for night time use. In certain tactical situations the use of the Benelli Super 90 semi-auto 12-gauge shotgun (considered the Rolls Royce of 12-gauge weapons) is handy and for barricaded subjects a dandy door lock or hinge defeater is the Smith and Wesson in a shortened pump action

During officer recovery exercises, SERT officers prepare to board a LAV for armored fire suppression. (Courtesy: Joe Savage/Portland PB-SERT)

SERT officers deploy from an Oregon National Guard LAV during officer recovery training. Enjoying close-knit ties to local military units, SERT officers are afforded excellent training opportunities denied to many other police tactical teams. (Courtesy: Joe Savage/Portland PB-SERT)

version loaded with "Shok Lok" shells. For riot-control situations, the Portland SERT has a variety of less than lethal weapons on hand, including the Royal Ordnance Arwen 37mm performs not only five shot capacity gas delivery but can be loaded with kinetic energy batons to reach out and touch someone. Also available in 37mm are several Smith and Wesson gas guns that use the stingballs and wooden dowels loads. Smith and Wesson shotguns can disperse troublemakers with bean bag and stingball rounds.

The most dangerous of all tactical situations is the dynamic entry. Hostage situations and high-risk warrant service demand long and arduous hours of training to hone the skills necessary for this very demanding work. For covert/stealth entry techniques are used to slowly and methodically enter and clear a location where an armed and dangerous felon is hidden. After time, talk, and tear gas have failed to extract a suspect, and it is time for the team to "go get 'em," covert/stealth entry techniques are deployed. Probably the second most used tactic by SERT it takes many hours of training to learn and use properly and safely. Threat angles and assessment is continuous as the team moves in a coordinated effort to dominate the interior, room by room until the suspect is found and arrested.

Recently, in July 1998, inmates housed in the Oregon Juvenile Justice Complex, rioted inside the facility (a jail for the most hardened juvenile criminals in the state) and held staff and other inmates hostage; armed with a small arsenal of home-made weapons, they barricaded themselves inside a secure section of the sprawling maximum security facility. Initially, the Multnomah County Sheriff's Office Corrections Division Corrections Emergency Response Team (CERT) was called in, but as the situation deteriorated, Portland SERT was also summoned. Entry into the facility was an arduous and demanding task. Bars had to be drilled out and steel doors and bars were forcibly extracted. Yet once the SERT officers were poised for a tactical assault, the outcome was all but

inevitable. In a lightning raid through the besieged tiers, SERT officers arrested the hostage-takers and rescued the hostages without loss of life or serious injury.

The SERT has also practiced and perfected the art of assaulting vehicles that can be used by a suspect to take or move hostages—and these include trains, planes and buses. The SERT, like many SWAT units in the United States and counter-terrorist teams throughout the world, has also trained in rescuing hostages on board aircraft, such as a Boeing 737. Terrorist concerns have opened doors to allow SERT to train with Federal and state law enforcement agencies of all kinds to perfect the intricacies of aircraft entry and assault and rescue—both of military and civilian craft. Other aspects of Portland Police Bureau SERT training includes: dignitary protection, rappelling, explosive entries, wooded movement/searches, high risk vehicle stops, security site surveys, defensive tactics and intensified tactical training with outside agencies.

SERT deploys five standard Chevrolet Caprice Police cruisers, unmarked, that are used as first responder vehicles. The SERT van is a large Grumman van designed for equipment storage and as a mobile command post. This van is driven to the scene and SERT personnel gather their equipment from it. The two officers assigned to SERT as intelligence officers use the van as a command post. The BART (Bureau Armored Rescue Truck) is a refurbished and reworked armored transport vehicle. Used for a bank delivery truck it was destined for destruction as law will not allow it to be sold. The armored BART is used for team delivery, hostage rescue, and as a very effective fortified door puller. Occasionally, when available for drug interdiction, the Oregon National Guard will deliver, complete with drivers, light armored vehicles (LAVs). These larger, faster vehicles are improved ballistically over BART and have great personnel delivery space and ability over rough terrain. Inside BART SERT carries a large assortment of breaching tools and body bunkers.

During training, Portland SERT officers deploy smoke, as well as diversionary devices. Note lead officer armed with the protective Body Bunker shield. (Courtesy: Joe Savage/Portland PB-SERT)

As a wounded officer is dragged to safety during Portland Police SERT rescue training, officers cover the withdrawal to safety with their Body Bunker shields. (Courtesy: Joe Savage/Portland PB-SERT)

Two Portland SERT officers pose for the camera in their special protective gear, worn while executing live-fire exercises with simulations. (Courtesy: Joe Savage/Portland PB-SERT)

Renown throughout the United States as one of the country's premier rope experts, SERT officers train and hone their climbing and rappelling skills with zealous dedication. (Courtesy: Joe Savage/Portland PB-SERT)

Officers prepare to deploy for a door pull on a drug location using BART (Bureau Armored Rescue Truck). Note hooks in place for the execution of the door pull. (Courtesy: Joe Savage/Portland PB-SERT)

Two SERT officers prepare to deploy from their "take-home" Chevy Caprice. Note cloth Portland Police Bureau shield affixed to the camouflaged flak vest. (Courtesy: Joe Savage/Portland PB-SERT)

The Portland Police Bureau SERT BART. (Courtesy: Joe Savage/Portland PB-SERT)

On the firing line with SERT officers and their MP5 submachine guns. (Courtesy: Joe Savage/Portland PB-SERT)

Urban Camouflage! A SERT sniper team (shooter and observer) prepares for a day at the range. (Courtesy: Joe Savage/Portland PB-SERT)

From the "it would suck to be him" file, a tight-grouping of 9mm holes lace a SERT target after a bust on the range. (Courtesy: Joe Savage/Portland PB-SERT)

Nice and tight, a SERT entry element prepares to execute a high-risk warrant. (Courtesy: Joe Savage/Portland PB-SERT)

The White Devils
The Alpini: Italy's Mountain Troops

Alberto Scarpitta

Described by one U.S. Army Special Forces officer as "cold weather commandos," the airborne-raiders from the Monte Cervino Alpine Paratroop Battalion are considered among NATO's elite.

Nestled behind a mountain boulder in the first few flakes of a snowstorm, the soldier was invisible in his white coveralls. Even his weapon, a Beretta SC-70/90 was concealed by strips of white tape fastened to the stock and barrel in a dizzying pattern. Peering through his field glasses, the soldier could see a column of men marching toward his position in a tired formation. The high altitude of Italy's Alps, after all, would take the breath away from the mightiest of warrior. As the column advanced through the narrow pass, supported by several jeeps, trapped by the majestic peaks, the soldier realized that any invader would face a difficult task in trying to fight his way through the Alps. Yet difficult wasn't impossible. That task fell to the Alpini—Italy's elite mountain commandos.

When the Cold War commenced, and the Soviet Union was seen as Europe's primary threat, defense officials in Rome realized that the most likely invasion route into Italy, should Europe once again be thrust into war, would be from the east, through the mountainous areas abutting her northern and north-eastern borders. Ravaged by war and burdened by a faltering economy, the Italian Defense undertook a bold program to achieve more with less and to defend the northern approaches with an elite force of soldier who could withstand, possibly even vanquish, an overwhelming foe. As a result, five Alpine Brigades were created—the "Taurinense," "Orobica," "Tridentina," "Cadore" and "Julia." The brigades were regional—both in areas of responsibility and the soldiers they recruited. All brigades ware strategically located: the "Taurinense" in North-Western Alps with 3rd Corps in Milan, the "Julia" with 5th Corps based at Vittorio Veneto and responsible for the defense of the north-eastern border with Austria and Yugoslavia, while the other three were responsible for the defense of the crucial Brenner Pass with 4th Corps based at Bolzano. Later, in the early sixties, all the alpine units were grouped under the head of the 4th Corps, which became the 4th Alpine Corps.

Each alpine brigade consisted of an Alpini regiment of three or four Alpini battalions, one mountain artillery regiment with three or four groups (battalions), signal and engineer companies, an aviation and a mountain-paratroopers platoon.

In addition each brigade had a Carabinieri (military police) platoon attached to it, a defensive battalion trained to fight from fixed defensive positions, and a logisticss group, responsible for supplying food, ammunition and equipment to the combat elements using off-road vehicles, sleds and even mules. In the mid-1960s, the alpine paratroopers platoons were grouped together, in order to form the elite Alpine Paratroop Company *"Compagnia Alpini Paracadutisti Monte Cervino."*

In 1975, the Italian military underwent an all-encompassing reorganization and the mountain regiments were disbanded, with the specialized infantry and artillery battalions being assigned directly to brigade headquarters. The brigades, interestingly enough, were maintained, but their overall operational strength was reduced by a debilitating thirty-percent. By the end of the Cold War, the alpine defense battalions, as well as the "Orobica" and "Cadore" Brigades, were also disbanded.

THE ALPINE TROOPS TODAY

The end of the Soviet Union brought to an end the potential that Europe would be embroiled in a full-scale war between the NATO and Warsaw Pact powers. For Italy, that meant that the threat to the northern frontiers was nullified. Yet the end of the Cold War brought about new conflict opportunities, as well as enormous military and security risks for Europe. The removal of a consistent threat and the ever greater attention on operations other than war led the Italian Army to a new deep reorganization, focusing attention on the building of an army of quality, small but well trained and armed, with high level of professionalism. In

A platoon commander from the Susa Battalion, AMF(L) Italian contingent, receives instructions from his company commander during combat training in woodland. Note the old all-green fatigues, still used in OPFOR training scenarios.

this new army alpine units had to continue to maintain itself as the NATO standard-bearer for all mountain troops. Under these guidelines the operative abilities of the army were divided into three "abilities packs": projection, reaction, presence and surveillance, all with different tasks and capabilities. The army, gearing toward becoming a professional force, would no longer rely on conscripts to carry the burden.

The forces of projection are fully staffed with VFB (volunteers on short-term service) and VFP (volunteers on permanent service) and are

Alpini troopers from the Tridentina Brigade during FIBUA training with MILES weapons effect simulators fitted to the old Beretta BM-59 7.62mm assault rifles.

A well camouflaged TOW launcher equipped with a Galileo thermal camera sight for night vision. Each Alpini regiment maintains six TOW launchers.

suited for operations "out of area" of peace support. The forces of reaction are intended as the Italian contribution to the NATO Rapid Reaction Corps, and are at this moment largely based on conscripts serving for ten months. As part of its modernization plan, the Italian Army is transforming these units to an all-professional force. The forces for presence and surveillance are composed of conscripts, are responsible for defensive operations *inside* Italy, though they may also be employed in disaster relief operations inside Italy, or to affected areas in the immediate regional area.

All the operative units are assigned to a new Operational Land Forces Command (COMFOTER) based in Verona, which operates through four division/corps-level intermediate headquarters, grouping three to four brigades, according to the specific required missions. All the Alpine units are grouped together under the *Comando Truppe Alpine* (COM T.A.), and are based at Bolzano, home of the 4th Alpine Corps. As a result of this all-encompassing reorganizational plan within the Italian military, the COM T.A. has brigades and sub-units belonging to all the three "abilities packs" and may be projected in part, thanks to the virtually professional Taurinense Brigade.

A battalion group of alpine operators is assigned to the Allied Command Europe Mobile Force (Land), responsible for the defense of the alliance's flanks. The AMF(L) component is regularly deployed in Norway as a reaction force, where good arctic and mountain skills are required. This Italian contingent usually comprises the Susa Alpini Battalion from 3rd Alpini Regiment, the 40th Mountain Artillery Battery belonging to the 1st Mountain Artillery Regiment, and the Taurinense Force Medical Unit.

The Minimi light machine gun is intended to provide fire support for the infantry squad. The 5.56mm NATO standard ammunition is usually fed in 200-round metal link belts but the weapon can use also the 30-round magazine of the SC 70/90 assault rifles.

Apart from this NATO contribution, Alpine troops participated in many multinational and autonomous national missions in recent years. The most important ones were in Mozambique, where the Susa Battalion and the alpine paratroopers were deployed from 1993 to 1994 in a difficult peace keeping operation, and in former Yugoslavia. In the Balkans, alpine units belonging to Taurinense Brigade regularly rotated with other army units as part of the Italian contingent of SFOR (Stabilization Force), formerly IFOR, with duties of monitoring the situation and control the inter-entity lines established by Dayton Accords.

A five men mortar squad from the Monte Cervino Alpine Paratroop Battalion moves into position in a rain swept valley in northern Italy.

Operators from the Monte Cervino Alpine Paratroop Battalion prepare to fire their 81mm mortar from a concealed firing position.

The OTO Melara M-56 105mm pack howitzer is a lightweight weapon which fires HE, smoke and illuminating rounds with a selection of seven different charges. The standard towing vehicle is the ubiquitous Iveco VM-90 light truck but the weapon is designed to break down into man-portable loads for transportation in very difficult terrain.

THE COMANDO TRUPPE ALPINE

The Alpine Troops Command consists of three alpine brigades (Taurinense, Julia and Tridentina), the Alpine Training Center, the Monte Cervino Alpine Paratroopers Battalion and additional corps assets: 2nd Signal Regiment, 2nd Engineers Regiment, 24th Logistics Regiment, 4th Army Aviation Regiment "Altair" and two infantry regiments (16th and 18th) which are recruits training centers for conscripts. Additional combat and service support units may be received directly from COMFOTER according to the mission and operational requirements.

The three brigades each have integral artillery, engineer and service elements, and beyond their traditional scope of expertise in winter and mountain warfare, are also trained in built-up area combat, as well as joint operations with armored and airmobile units. The brigade organization is the same: one command and combat supports group, three battalion-sized Alpini (alpine infantry) regiments, one mountain artillery regiment, one logistics battalion and a field hospital. The Taurinense Brigade is stationed in the north-west of Italy, with 2nd and 3rd Alpini Regiments and the 1st Mountain Artillery Regiment as main combat support element. The Julia Brigade is based in the north-eastern corner of Italy, along with the 7th, 8th and 14th Alpini Regiments, plus the 3rd Mountain Artillery Regiment. The Tridentina Brigade is stationed in the Brenner Pass area, and consists of the 5th, 11th, and 6th Alpini Regiments and the 5th Mountain Artillery Regiment.

All the brigade command and combat supports groups are composed of the headquarters section, headquarters company, supporting the command post, signal and engineer companies. The latter is composed of HQ and service platoon, three combat engineer platoons and one heavy equipment platoon and provides combat engineer support: demolition, mine laying and clearance, bridging, earth moving works, water supply, and route maintenance.

THE ALPINI REGIMENTS

The Alpine infantry regiments are organized into command and service company and a single battalion, with a small headquarters, three rifle company and one support weapons company. The rifle companies possess a HQ platoon, three thirty-man rifle platoons, each consisting of four squads of seven soldiers. An antitank platoon is equipped with six Milan antitank missile launchers. The rifle companies are designed to be light infantrymen in every sense of the word—they are tasked with being able to carry with them everything they'll need in combat, from a change of underwear to Milan ATGWs. However, these units are also equipped with a fleet of Iveco VM-90 light trucks that can resupply the force

Although the Minimi has become the Alpini's standard squad support weapon, the MG-42/59 7.62mm light machine gun is still present in a sustained fire role, though, as seen here, primarily mounted on Alpini vehicles.

The alpine infantry regiments from both the Taurinense and Julia Brigades are scheduled to receive eighteen Puma 6x6 APCs each for use in peace support missions. Monte Cervino Battalion will receive the shorter 4x4 version of the same vehicle.

The air defense battery of the mountain artillery regiments fields the LPD-20 warning radar.

Alpini troopers on parade—skilled specialists capable of performing where most cannot survive.

Alpini troopers in full winter gear parade through the streets of a northern Italian town. Note the gray-green felt mountaineer's hat adorned with golden cap badge for officers and NCOs, and black for other ranks.

Monte Cervino Alpine Paratroop Battalion operators glide to earth on a mountain clearing after a static-line jump "behind enemy lines" during OPFOR exercises.

during lengthy deployments. Future plans by the Italian military also call for Alpini forces to be equipped with Puma 6x6 wheeled APCs—especially when deployed overseas on dangerous peace-keeping assignments. The support weapons company has two heavy mortars platoons with four 120mm mortars each, and one TOW missile-equipped antitank platoon of six firing posts mounted on light vehicles or on Swedish BV-206 tracked all terrain vehicles. The regiment is organized into a flexible configuration that can function and fight from squad-sized elements up to a combined battalion task force. Alpine infantry battalions can maneuver with speed and surprise in all types of terrain and climatic conditions, day or night.

Alpini forces are equipped with standard special forces equipment and weaponry. The standard-issue personal weapon is the Beretta SC-70/90 5.56mm assault rifle, while every rifle squad has a Minimi 5.56mm light machine gun and one Panzerfaust-3 antitank weapon. The MG-42/59 7.62mm light machine gun is also carried by squad for added support, as well as mounted to the unit's trucks and other vehicles.

Standard-issue winter combat clothing consists of a Gore-Tex windproof smock and trousers is worn over thermal underclothes. A white camouflaged two-pieces snow suit is worn over the combat kit if required. Not waterproof, the snow suits help the men blend into the surroundings providing excellent camouflage in the snow.

BRIGADE SUPPORT UNITS

The mountain artillery regiment fields HQ and headquarters and service battery, one light artillery group (battalion) with three batteries, each equipped with eight OTO Melara M-56 105mm howitzers specially designed for mountain warfare. The battalion also maintains antiaircraft capabilities with one air defense battery equipped with twelve short-range Stinger surface-to-air-missiles.

The logistics battalion is responsible for the provision of combat supplies, ammunition, fuel, rations and other material, for brigade equipment maintenance and furnishes additional transport capabilities. The battalion is divided into four companies: (a) the headquarters and service company; (b) the transport company responsible for the force's trucks and fleet of BV-206 all-terrain tracked vehicles; (c); the ordnance company; and, (d) the maintenance company. A medical unit gives second-line support to the medical personnel within the brigade, though at the time of this article's writing, only the Taurinense Brigade fields an active medical force; other brigades field reserve medical teams.

EAGLE FEATHER

All ranks in the command, with the exception of the army aviation regiment, are instantly recognizable by the famous gray-green felt mountaineer's hat worn with a black eagle feather and a colored tassel on the left-hand side. Both feather and pompon are also worn on the Kevlar

Striking photograph of a squad of Alpini troopers, completely camouflaged for the snow and mountainous conditions, all armed with the Beretta SC-70/90 5.56mm assault rifles.

Urban warfare in the mountains! An Alpini trooper, whose fatigues, face and SC70/90 assault rife is meticulously camouflaged, prepares to storm a machine gun nest during live-fire exercises.

helmet—even in combat conditions. The black metal cap badge depicts an eagle above a light infantry bugle containing the regimental number. All ranks wear a green metal collar patch.

Alpine units, apart from the Taurinense Brigade, consist largely of conscripts undergoing their national service. Most of them are local men born and bred in the mountain areas and are used to the demanding work required of an Alpini trooper—all are physically fit, highly motivated and, after a brief military training regimen, capable of surviving and fighting in the difficult cold-weather high-altitude environment in which they operate. Conscripts spend a few weeks in a Conscript Training Regiment and then are assigned to their active unit, where they undergo a further four months of advanced squad and platoon training.

Italian draftees serve a total of ten months, creating a significant degree of what many Italian officers have described as "turbulence" within the units. This is, however, balanced in part by the fact that under the conscription system a large number of men are trained and could in an emergency be recalled to the colors of their parent regiments. Many continue to live and work in the mountain areas, retaining their fitness and mountain skills.

The *Associazione Nazionale Alpini*, or ANA, groups former Alpini returned to civilian life who want to maintain alpine military customs and traditions even in civilian life and preserve their ties with active alpine units. As with many units of the Italian slimmed-down armed forces, some alpine units have more than one "hat" to be worn.

The Taurinense Brigade, for example, is composed primarily of professionals, and forms part of the "projection pack" and could be called upon to respond to purely national requirements. At the same time its contribution to AMF(L) makes the brigade part of the "reaction pack" with a NATO context as a light-infantry mountain elite to serve as a rapid deployment force to any regional hot-spot. It was recently announced that the Julia Brigade will become a framework formation with Hungarian and Slovenian infantry battalions assigned to it. Hungarian and Slovenian

Ideally camouflaged for operations in the snow-laced approaches to a mountain in northern Italy, an Alpini operator peers through the sights of his Beretta M70/78 5.56mm light machine gun while maintaining his balance with a forty kilogram pack on his back.

Winter training in the Alps—Alpini style. A squad of troopers moves silently and quickly through the deep snow banks.

Moving cautiously up a steep ravine, Alpini troopers provide a 180° field of fire with their SC 70/90 assault rifles.

officers are being integrated into the brigade headquarters and the new trinational brigade will be ready for peace-keeping assignments and disaster relief operations.

The Tridentina Brigade could have an international mission in the future, providing a regiment for a proposed German-Italian mountain infantry brigade. The plans for this new multinational unit are in the early planning stages but many feel that the force will become operational no later than 2001.

THE MONTE CERVINO ALPINE PARATROOP BATTALION

The Monte Cervino Alpini Paratroop Battalion is a special-forces capable unit reporting directly to the Command of Alpine Troops in Bolzano. It consists of one headquarters and service company, and two mountain-paratroopers companies. Each airborne company possesses a command platoon, two rifle platoons with three rifle squads and one antitank squad with two Milan launchers, a third platoon that will be transformed into an armored scout platoon of four Puma light armored wheeled vehicles and one medium mortars platoon with three 81mm mortars. One company is built solely on volunteers and professional soldiers, while the other relies on an elite cadre of conscripts. The training regimen for the force is arduous, and is personified by the unit's motto "*Mai Strac*," Italian for "never tired." The battalion is afforded great access to transport aircraft and choppers and is reported to jump well over fifty times a year—both static line and free-fall.

A specialized regimen for the battalion includes mountain climbing training, winter training, ski and sled proficiency, long-range patrol and reconnaissance techniques in arctic conditions, as well as intensive cold-weather survival instruction. In the battalion, one platoon per company is trained to deploy by free-fall jumps through ram air chutes. The battalion's officers and NCO are all sent to the Harvard University of military patrol schools, the acclaimed NATO International Long Range Patrol School at Pfullendorf (Germany), and they are also sent to arctic survival courses in Sweden and Norway, and to other military schools in the United States (Ranger Course) and Germany.

The battalion also maintains close operational links to the legendary Italian airborne special operations commando force, the 9th "Colonel Moschin" Assault Paratroop Regiment, though the Alpini unit is not designed to become a mountain-warfare clone of this airborne raiding force. Battalion operators are armed exclusively with the Beretta SCP 70/90 5.56mm assault rifle.

In a striking contrast to the pristine beauty of the Italian Alps, Alpini troopers set to fire their 120mm smoothbore mortar. The support weapons companies each fields two mortar platoons.

The Hägglunds BV-206 all terrain vehicles provide versatile transport for heavy support weapons and equipment.

THE ALPINE TRAINING CENTER

The Alpine Training Center at Aosta, in northwest Italy, is responsible for mountain training for officers, non-commissioned officers and volunteers assigned to alpine troops. Courses for volunteers focus on basic instruction in military skiing, rock climbing, snowbound operations, rope techniques, first aid and rescue, and mountain combat operations. Officers and NCOs receive additional training in order to be able to pass their skills to their men, directing and managing all the mountain, climbing and military ski training in the active units.

Summer training is divided into seven weeks basic and seven weeks advanced courses in climbing techniques, leading to qualification of "Climbing and Mountain Warfare Military Instructor" and then, after further advanced training, as "First-Class Instructor." Winter training begins with ski practice taking place concurrently with training in the combat problems associated with winter warfare in the mountains. Climbing on ice and snow and avalanches security measures are also taught with zealous attention; this training lasts fourteen weeks (seven of basic and seven of advanced courses).

An AVES AB-205 helicopter from the 4th Army Aviation Regiment "Altair" lands in a mountain clearing during combat exercise in northern Italy.

An Alpini trooper monitors an enemy vehicle through the sights of his TOW ATGW launcher during live-fire exercises in northern Italy.

Alpine paratroopers were involved to the "Albatros" peace-keeping mission in Mozambique. Note green fatigues, BM-59 7.62mm assault rifle and UN blue helmets with Alpini eagle feather.

A conscript "Alpino" from the Taurinense Brigade poses for the camera in his United Nations blue beret and Italian "Middle Eastern" camouflage scheme. The brigade participated in "Operation Albatros" in Mozambique from 1993 to 1994.

An Alpini trooper scans a roadway during SFOR operations near Pale. The 3rd and 9th Alpini Regiments contributed to SFOR operations in the former Yugoslavia.

An Alpini trooper posts guard duty at the headquarters of the Italian brigade in Sarajevo. The flak vest is the heavy bullet-proof "Corazza 2," standard-issue among elite combat units in the Italian military.

Alpini troopers stand guard at the Pale crossroads during a SFOR mission.

Wearing his uncharacteristic woodland-pattern camouflage fatigues in the midst of a Bosnian winter, an Alpini trooper mans a defensive post in front of his Iveco vehicle during SFOR-duty. Note German-style long peaked cap with all uniforms, including combat clothing.

During an SFOR patrol, Alpini Iveco VM-90 light trucks and VM-90P move forward near hostile lines.

The famous black eagle feather, worn even on Kevlar helmets in combat, as seen on an Alpini trooper manning a front-line position in Bosnia during a SFOR deployment.

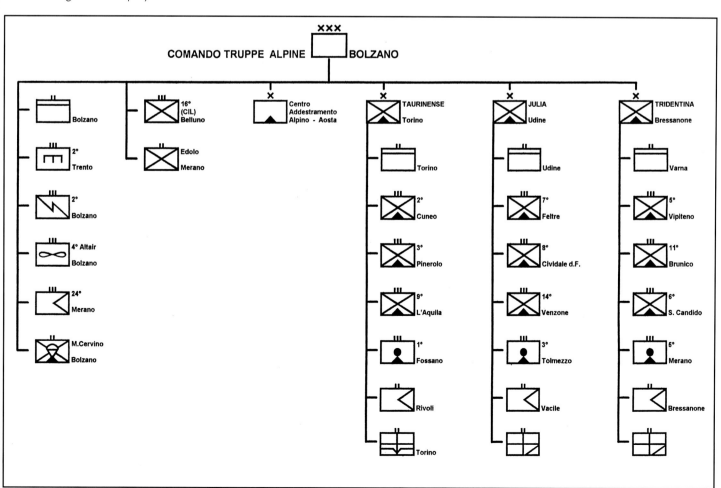

COMANDO TRUPPE ALPINE — BOLZANO

Bolzano

2° Trento

2° Bolzano

4° Altair Bolzano

24° Merano

M.Cervino Bolzano

16° (CIL) Belluno

Edolo Merano

Centro Addestramento Alpino - Aosta

TAURINENSE Torino

Torino

2° Cuneo

3° Pinerolo

9° L'Aquila

1° Fossano

Rivoli

Torino

JULIA Udine

Udine

7° Feltre

8° Cividale d.F.

14° Venzone

3° Tolmezzo

Vacile

TRIDENTINA Bressanone

Varna

5° Vipiteno

11° Brunico

6° S. Candido

5° Merano

Bressanone

SLOVAK SWAT
A New Breed of Super Cop for Eastern Europe

Gilles Rivet

Proud of their young nation and of their unique unit esprit de corps, UOU officers pose with the Slovak flag.

To the men wearing black coveralls and clutching their MP5 submachine guns, the reality that they were in seemed surreal. After all, only ten years earlier, the very thought of heavily-armed police officers racing through the streets of Bratislava on a high-risk warrant to arrest heroin smugglers would have been unheard of. Citizens in Czechoslovakia feared the police—they didn't challenge them to gun battles. But the world has changed beyond reason in the course of a decade. A New World Order has set it, one that has replaced rigid Communist rule with a free-market free-for-all that has seen Eastern Europe turn into a Chicago of the 1920s. Yet this new breed of gangster would make Al Capone shudder. Cruelty and savage violence aren't required tools of the trade—they are a code of behavior and a way of life. Criminals no longer hold up banks with pistols—they rob with RPGs.

To combat this explosive and, some fear, impossible-to-stop criminal reality, the nations of the former Eastern Bloc have had to evaluate and mobilize their police departments for a war the likes of which had never been waged on the streets of the continent.

In a remote section of a Bratislava suburb, the morning quiet is shattered by an ear-splitting explosion that shatters some windows and rocks the sidewalk like a small earthquake. A building under construction has been chosen by a select group of Slovakian top-cops as the site of a day's worth of tubular assault training. The explosion, a small charge that turned a wooden door into a fragmented mess of splinters, was an opening salvo in a dynamic entry meant to flush a location with a heavily armed stream of law enforcement. In a flash of movement, ten men, all in black, race into a five-room flat, weapons at the ready, clearing rooms in delicate dance of cover, conceal, and advance. One by one the rooms are cleared. The assault takes all of forty-five seconds.

For the next twelve hours, operators from the Slovak Police counter-terrorist team, the *Utvar Osobitneho Urcenia*, or UOU, will rock the Bratislava neighborhood with Semtex, diversionary devices and small arms fire. The reality of the new state, which together with the Czech Republic split from what was once Czechoslovakia, is that many of the

freedoms that the end of communism has brought have also come with a steep price tag. For the UOU, a unit that was formed to combat hijackers and suicidal terrorists, the bread-and-butter of their operational existence is battling organized crime. According to one UOU operator, "In Slovakian Republic, we have very little experience concerning the political terrorism as it exists in the West. Acts perpetrated by the religious movements from the Middle East, or any other faction, are unheard of here. Our call-outs, now averaging two a week, deal solely with the criminal element. In reality, the Slovak Police does not need to battle a determined terrorist army. The criminals, even juvenile gangs, are armed with assault rifles and explosives. The UOU wages a dedicated campaign against heavily defended clandestine immigration rings, prostitution and white slavery operations, gunrunning, and of course, narcotic rings.

SELECTION AND PRACTICE

The UOU is the elite of the Slovakian Police and a strictly volunteer force. Before being even allowed to submit one's request to try out for the unit, an officer must have at least three years on the force, must possess and exemplary work jacket, and must pass a grueling set of interviews and psychological profiles. Once a police officer is deemed fit for volunteering into the unit, he undergoes a series of harsh, and sometimes brutal, physical tests meant to weed out all candidates who might not survive the three months of training. This phase is concluded with a notorious five-day training scenario where the officer is literally on his feet for some 120 hours—the purpose of the soft-core torture is to force a class of wannabe's to learn to function as a single cohesive team. The UOU is not looking for lone mavericks. The unit is centered on it being a team, with each piece interchangeable with the next and no one individual more important than his partners.

UOU commanders realize that they are one of the premier police tactical teams in all Eastern Europe, but their operational ambitions are limited by the harsh financial restrictions of the Slovakian Republic. Training time is limited and overtime virtually unheard of. Even on the range, the officers are ordered to be frugal with ammunition. Much of the

From an ideal observation post overlooking St. Michael's castle and much of Bratislava, a UOU sniper team keeps a beat on their target with their Swiss-produced SIG SG-3000 5.56mm rifle.

unit's combat obstacle course was built by unit officers, on their own time and with their individually-purchased raw materials. Nevertheless, the unit does manage to train on aircraft under repair, trains in yards undergoing maintenance, and a bus whenever the opportunity permits.

The esprit de corps in the UOU is impressive and clearly only those who truly want to be in the unit wear the black Nomex coveralls into action. Officers must re-qualify on the range and on the obstacle course every six months in order to retain their spot in the unit. Shooting skills are perfected zealously. All UOU operators, interestingly enough, are

All UOU are cross-trained as snipers—a luxury that allows sniper and observer teams to change roles during lengthy deployments and call-outs. Here, atop a Bratislava roof, a UOU sniper peers through the sights of his SIG SG-3000 5.56mm rifle, as his trusted observer searches for additional targets with his field glasses.

cross-trained as snipers.

Because training facilities are so primitive in Slovakia, the UOU frequently sends its officers overseas for "advanced" instruction. "This allows our men to discover some new materials but also of the new techniques of tactical entries and raids," claims one UOU officer. "We can also exchange our information and our experiences. It is a fabulous means to progress. We have worked with Americans, French, Italian, Hungarians and Austrians. Our goal is to establish relations with similar teams in neighboring countries in order to establish an operational network."

Like virtually all police tactical teams in Europe, and the world, the primary weapon of the UOU is the Heckler and Koch family of MP5 9mm submachine guns—especially the MP5A3. All officers carry the Czech-produced CZ75 9mm handgun—considered by many to be the best designs to emerge from Europe since 1945. Interestingly enough, for a unit that suffers from financial restrictions, the UOU's primary sniper weapon is the Swiss-produced SIG SG-3000 5.56mm rifle.

The future promises busy days ahead for the UOU. Slovakia has been hit by a serious economic crises that ravages much of the country and opens a good portion of society to the temptations and tentacles of organized crime. UOU operators see themselves as a long black-clad frontier, propping up the thin blue line that maintains law and order in a fledgling democracy.

A UOU sniper tandem keeps their eyes—and weapon—trained on a pair of suspects during training exercise in Bratislava.

At a construction site in Bratislava turned into an impromptu training ground, a UOU operator is ready to move quickly toward his target with MP5 in hand.

Taking cover behind a wall, a masked UOU officers shouts "Police, Drop Your Weapons!" as he places a suspect in the sites of his CZ75.

The chaos, fear and confusion of a dynamic entry with stun devices and smoke—a UOU entry team negotiates a blinding cloud of smoke as they attempt to clear an apartment.

The unmistakable tap on the back—indicating to the lead officer that it is safe to proceed. The UOU utilizes standard SWAT practices and signals—a direct result of their training with similar teams in Western Europe and the United States.

With his MP5 in hand, UOU operators order a "suspect" onto the ground.

During tubular assault training in Bratislava, a UOU entry team prepares to race into a targeted location.

Stoic portrait of UOU operators lined up on a stairway—ready to assault a simulated narcotics location during training exercises in Bratislava.

With their MP5s at the ready, UOU operator carefully peel around a staircase, careful not to be ambushed by criminal elements who are often armed better than them.

Takedown UOU style! During tubular assault training, a UOU team subdues and cuffs a prisoner—one of their own who pulled the short straw and was forced to play "the perp."

A menacing equation to any Slovak criminal gang—the long black line of UOU officers coming their way.

During assault training exercises, a UOU cover team prepares itself to provide an entry element with a wall of blanketing 9mm fire.

Three UOU officers present the business-end of their MP5 9mm submachine guns.

Racing in the open, careful not to be in the cross-hairs of a drug dealer's AK-47, a UOU operator moves into firing position.

A Mafioso's worst nightmare and perhaps Slovakia's only hope of emerging from a lethal crime-wave: a UOU officer at work.

After a full day of tactical training near Bratislava, a UOU operator poses for the camera and displays his gear and kit.